Collected Plays

Copyright © 1952, 1953, 1954, 1960, 1968 by Gregory Corso

Copyright © 2021 by the Literary Estate of Gregory Corso,
Sheri Langerman Baird, Executor

Intoduction copyright © 2021 by Rick Schober

Back cover photo of Gregory Corso, Paris, 1957 by Allen Ginsberg.
Copyright © 2021 by The Allen Ginsberg LLC. All rights reserved.

ISBN 978-0-578-77701-6

Tough Poets Press
Arlington, Massachusetts 02476
U.S.A.

www.toughpoets.com

COLLECTED PLAYS

Gregory Corso

Tough Poets Press
Arlington, Massachusetts

Contents

Introduction

Some Notes on Corso's Plays

Readers who have ventured this deeply into the bibliography of Gregory Corso (1930–2001) are no doubt aware of his prominence among post-World War II poets, as well as his role in launching and popularizing the Beat movement in American literature in the 1950s along with writers Jack Kerouac, Allen Ginsberg, and William Burroughs. Not so well known is that, in addition to several volumes of poetry, Corso also wrote a novel (*The American Express*, Olympia Press, 1961) and several plays and play fragments, only a few of which have been previously published.

Putting together an accurate chronology of Corso's plays is virtually impossible. In his writings, he alluded to three separate plays as being his first. In a 1956 letter to poet Randall Jarrell and his wife Mary, Corso referred to *The Death of a Beautiful Boy* as "a play I wrote sometime ago, in fact my first play." His 1968 handwritten note on the 108-page typescript of the play held in the Special Collections Library at Stony Brook University reads as follows:

> *This is the only extant copy of final play — by me,*
> *Gregory Corso — I do not wish any of this to be*
> *published or performed while I live & die — as I*
> *consider this a terrible yet soul-draining effort —*

Respecting his wishes, the play is not included in this collection.

In a 1978 letter to New Directions publisher James Laughlin about the possibility of having a collection of four of his mid-1950s plays published, Corso wrote, "I think recalling that I had mentioned a play, my first, about 12 pages, *Sarpedon*, 1954, in verse." Between 1954 and 1955, Corso was living covertly in Eliot House at Harvard University. Previously, he had been living in a $5-a-week room at nearby 12 Ash Street Place but was forced out when the City of Cambridge informed the house's owner that he could not legally rent out rooms. At the time, classics professor John H. Finley, Jr. was Master of Eliot House and, according to his prefatory comments to a 1978 reading of *Sarpedon* at the Naropa Institute, Corso was told by one of Finley's teaching assistants that he would be allowed to stay if he could write a Greek play. "I did it overnight," he said.

Sarpedon was first published by Tough Poets Press in 2016. The version reproduced in this volume has been corrected from that previous edition.

To further complicate the early chronology, there is yet another play that Corso had referred to as his first. The *Untitled Play* that opens this collection is an "unpublished, abandoned," although seemingly complete, work held in the archives of the Harry Ransom Center at the University of Texas at Austin. Corso's handwritten note at the top of this piece states "1952, earliest work, only copy."

Corso's first published play, *In This Hung-Up Age, A One-Act Farce Written in 1954*, appeared in the U.K. in the January 1962 issue of *Encounter*. It was subsequently reprinted with minor edits and Americanized spelling in *New Directions in Prose and Poetry 18* (1964) and *The Kenning Anthology of Poets Theater: 1945–1985* (2010). It is this version I have chosen to reprint here. The New Theatre Workshop's April 28, 1955 performance of the play was considered "a minor triumph" by a *Harvard Crimson* reviewer who wrote that "The language of his characters is fast, vigorous, and funny, and the denouement is grotesquely original." And, "Its humor and its design are blunt; it elicits spontaneous enthusiasm." In his notes on the play, Corso wrote, "I can safely claim that this play, indeed document, pre-dates anything ever written about the Hipster and hip-talk, the Square, and the advent of San Francisco's 'poesy rebirth.'"

Standing on a Streetcorner, A Little Play, illustrated by Corso, appeared in the March–April 1962 edition of *Evergreen Review*. A manuscript for the play held in the Kenneth Spencer Research Library at the University of Kansas indicates that the play was written in 1953 and originally titled *Standing on the Street Corner*. Another play, *A Prehistoric Day*, also held in the Spencer Research Library, was written in 1953 according to Corso's note on his manuscript. It is a short comedy about an attempted drug deal involving a sloth, a sabre-toothed tiger, a mammoth, and a giant lizard. Unfortunately, the entire play was handwritten and Corso's penmanship is challenging. The majority of this work was undecipherable to me and, as such, it has not been included in this volume.

JFK, A Little Verse Play was "written in Greece 1960 after hearing the acceptance speech of John F Kennedy following the nomination." Corso's handwritten note on the first page of the typescript held at the Harry Ransom Center and reproduced in this volume states that it was his third and final draft. In a 1962 letter to James Laughlin, Corso proposed a collection of his plays and essays, which he suggested might make "a varied and interesting and fine little book." All of the works he mentioned had been previously published, with the exception of the JFK play, which he then referred to as *President Kennedy*.

There is little documentation about the origins of *That Little Black Door on the Left*. It is not mentioned in *An Accidental Autobiography: The Selected Letters of Gregory Corso* (2003), although it was most likely written in the mid-1960s. It appears in the book *Pardon Me, Sir, But Is My Eye Hurting Your Elbow?*, a collection of short screenplays published in 1968 and illustrated by *Mad Magazine* cartoonist Mort Drucker. The collection was described as "a comic examination of the hypocrisies, dishonesties, and ironies of American life as seen though the eyes of twelve of America's greatest young writers." Among the other contributors were Terry Southern, Allen Ginsberg, and Bruce Jay Freidman. According to the original editor's note, *That Little Black Door* was to be "filmed without dialogue. All of the performances will be pantomime. The only sound track will be musical." The Internet Movie Database (IMDb) states that the film version of *Pardon Me, Sir* was never produced due to its "questionable taste."

Finally, there is *Way Out, A Poem in Discord*, written in 1956 and published by Bardo Matrix, Kathmandu, Nepal, in 1974. Writing in the May/June 1995 issue of *New Observations*, publisher Ira Cohen called it "more play than poem" and mentioned that it was, in fact, performed once, at the Yak & Yeti Crystal Ballroom on October 11, 1974. Like *The Death of a Beautiful Boy*, this piece was essentially disowned by Corso. In letters to Allen Ginsberg and poet John Weiners written between 1956 and 1957, he refers to the poem as "phony," "nowhere really," and "fucked up." Further, in a letter regarding his forthcoming 1958 City Lights collection of poems, *Gasoline*, he told publisher Lawrence Ferlinghetti, "I'm happy you won't use *Way Out*." For these reasons, and because it lacks the humorous spirit of his other plays, *Way Out* has not been included in this collection.

Many thanks are extended to Raymond Foye and George Scrivani for their editorial suggestions, stellar proofreading, and general guidance in preparing this collection.

Rick Schober

Untitled Play

Unpublished, Abandoned Work (1952)

Hedy's house. A large guest room expensively furnished with lamps and bookcases, a tea table in the middle of the room, and a huge sofa and five armchairs. There is a lighted fireplace, and a sword hanging directly above it.

Mudd, Leda, Peggy, Hedy's guests, are conversing. There is a knock on the door. Paul, Hedy's servant, walks to the door, opens it, and in enters Mr. Blots, an expected guest.

MUDD: *(Rising from the sofa, greeting Mr. Blots)* Ah, here you are, Blots. Where's your son? That darling chap—where is he?

BLOTS: Busy.

MUDD: Busy! How, busy? It's Sunday! Busy doing what?

BLOTS: Rot.

HEDY: Did you say, rot?

LEDA: I pray not.

BLOTS: I tied my son to a willow tree in a woodland known to no one but me.

MUDD: Clever. Clever.

BLOTS: And I took his clothes from him and left him there to rot, forever!

LEDA: Never!

HEDY: The man's obviously insane!

PEGGY: Or just plain mundane.

HEDY: Mr. Blots, it's against the law!

BLOTS: Haw-haw.

LEDA: Sir, the terror of the night is too much for any child to endure . . . especially if a father leaves him there to . . . rot.

HEDY: Mr. Mudd, you must demand he release his son!

MUDD: Miss Hedy, no sooner said than done.

BLOTS: *(Addressing all)* Deserves him right. He cries too much at night. He doesn't eat his squash . . .

MUDD: *(Being pushed on by Hedy)* Hogwash, Blots. I demand you tell us the whereabouts of your son!

LEDA: *(Whispers to Mudd)* Well done.

MUDD: Come now, Blots, tell us.

HEDY: Yes. Do so.

LEDA: Yes.

PEGGY: Yes.

BLOTS: No!

Enter Paul

PAUL: Tea is ready, Miss Hedy.

HEDY: *(To all, apologetically)* I regret to say there's no coffee today. *(To Paul)* Paul, bring out the mixed-nuts.

Exit Paul

MUDD: I do hope the tea is iced.

LEDA: So do I.

PEGGY: I do hope the nuts are spiced.

BLOTS: So do I.

HEDY: Mr. Blots, you are not welcomed to snack with us unless . . .

BLOTS: Yes?

HEDY: Unless you release your child.

Enter Paul, with nuts

PAUL: Miss Hedy, do you notice how artfully the nuts are piled?

HEDY: Splendid, Paul.

MUDD: The tea *is* iced.

LEDA: Yum-yum.

PEGGY: The nuts *are* spiced.

BLOTS: I want some.

HEDY: You'll get nothing of the kind unless you change your mind.

PAUL: Shall I throw him out, Miss Hedy?

HEDY: Paul, steady.

LEDA: Eeeek!

MUDD: Heavens, girl, what's up? . . . speak!

LEDA: *(Pointing toward the rug)* There . . . on the rug!

PEGGY: Good Lord . . . a bug!

HEDY: Where did it come from? Paul!

PAUL: Miss Hedy, you call?

HEDY: Yes *(points to rug)* . . . that, where did it come from?

PAUL: Ugh . . . a bug! I know not from where or whence it came, Miss Hedy.

HEDY: Well, just don't stand there . . . get rid of it!

PAUL: But, how?

MUDD: With your hand . . . squash it.

PAUL: My hand?

PEGGY: Oh, you can always wash it.

HEDY: Use a paper, a hankie . . . anything, just get rid of it!

BLOTS: No—I forbid it! A bug is a harmless creature. Just leave it; it'll go on its way.

HEDY: That's for *you* to say! I say squash it, squeeze it; any thing, just get it out of my house!

MUDD: Have you any flint, Miss Hedy? We can douse it.

PEGGY: It is an ugly thing, isn't it?

LEDA: Does it sting?

MUDD: It seems as it might;—wonder what it's called?

LEDA: Who cares!

HEDY: Paul . . . do away with it.

PAUL: Miss Hedy, I'm appalled! I have an extreme distaste for animals. Just the sight of them makes me frightfully ill. I tell you, Miss Hedy, I'm already ill!

BLOTS: Oh, be still. This, in the first place, is not an animal, but an insect.

PEGGY: Well, what did you expect, a kangaroo on the rug?

BLOTS: No . . . a bug.

LEDA: Eeeek . . . it moves!

BLOTS: Which further proves my theory. Just let it go on its way.

HEDY: What way? Right now it's headed toward mother's room. Mother's room! . . . she'll have a fit . . . we've got to stop it!

PEGGY: Here. Take this book.

HEDY: What's this for?

PEGGY: Just go over to it . . . and drop it.

HEDY: No. I couldn't. It's not in me.

BLOTS: Even if it were in you, you shouldn't. It's disgusting

. . . such a poor defenseless creature . . .

LEDA: Listen to teacher, here. You hypocrite! What about your poor boy rotting out there without help or clothes or anything?

MUDD: Blots, you're as base as a two-penny ring.

HEDY: You're as vile as an opiate.

PAUL: A mere thug, would be more appropriate.

LEDA: Eeeek! . . . the bug, it's gone!

HEDY: But where to?

PEGGY: To the beyon'.

The mother screams off stage, then comes rushing in and faints in the middle of the room.

HEDY: *(Rushing to her mother)* Mother! *(To Paul)* Quick, the salts!

Exit Paul

LEDA: Oh, dear! It's all our faults.

MUDD: How vulgar! . . . a home isn't safe with those things running loose.

PEGGY: My deah . . . you must call an exterminator the first thing tomorrow.

HEDY: Oh, what's the use? Mother'll be dead tomorrow.

PEGGY: No she won't. She just fainted, that's all.

MUDD: *(Patting the mother's hands)* Madam. Madam. We're not acquainted, but I do want to extend my deepest sorrow . . . good Lord, she is dead!

LEDA: She was stung!

Enter Paul, with the salts

PAUL: The salts, Miss Hedy.

MOTHER: *(Breathing heavily)* I was sitting there . . . rocking like I always rock, when suddenly I felt this—this thing creep up my legs *(She goes into a swoon; she is given more salts.)* Then—then I did the most natural thing it was in my power to do; I gave my leg a smack; o-o-o-h! I heard it squash, and felt it smear all over me!

BLOTS: You mean to say, madam, you killed the poor innocent creature without having any knowledge of what it was like?

MOTHER: My only impulse was to strike!

HEDY: Mr. Blots—a bug is a bug; one does not question its personality.

BLOTS: So I gather.

MUDD: Well, such is the casualty. Although I am inclined to feel that Mr. Blots, here grieves dearly for it.

Everyone laughs sarcastically.

BLOTS: Laugh—yes, laugh—someday the insects of the world will seek out their revenge . . . watch out!

everyone of you, watch out!

LEDA: How absurd!

PAUL: You're just too-too.

HEDY: I won't hear another word!

MOTHER: Who is this fellow, Hedy?

HEDY: A vile person, mother. A torturer of children.

MOTHER: Since when? Certainly he loves insects! . . . I can't believe he'd harm children . . .

PAUL: The truth could be that he's even killed them!

MOTHER: Heavens! Who invited him?

MUDD: I did, Madam—I thought him as good as most chaps.

MOTHER: Perhaps. But it seems poor judgment on your part. And who are you, by the by?

HEDY: This is Mr. Mudd, mother.

MOTHER: Mudd? Mudd? Not Ephraim Mudd's brother?

MUDD: Yes.

MOTHER: Well, bless my soul!

LEDA: Eeeek! . . . There . . . there in the nut bowl!

MUDD: Heavens, another bug!

The mother faints, Hedy gives her salts

PEGGY: All right, now, let's all keep our heads.

PAUL: It's quite small.

MUDD: What kind is it?

BLOTS: The kind that comes from beds.

HEDY: Are you implying that my beds are ridden with bedbugs?

BLOTS: I am. They're hidden in the springs and mattresses.

PEGGY: Also in shoes, hats and dresses.

HEDY: I don't believe it!

BLOTS: As sure as I am standing here, I proclaim it to be a bedbug, and it can only come from one place, your bed.

HEDY: My bed?

BLOTS: That's what I said.

HEDY: How dare you, sir?

PAUL: Let me throw him out, Miss Hedy.

HEDY: Steady. Steady. (*She kneels beside her mother*)

MUDD: I shall dispose of the creature! *(All eyes look upon him in admiration. He goes into a sort of heroics, until he approaches the bug, then he whisks out a hankie and picks it up, keeping it far away from him with his head turned. His face is pained as if the bug smelled. He then flicks it into the fireplace, hankie and all. There's a short burst of applause.)*

HEDY: I don't know how to thank you, Mr. Mudd.

MUDD: 'Twas nothing . . . nothing . . . as simple as plucking a rose bud.

PAUL: You were splendid, sir.

MUDD: Tut-tut. Nothing a-tall.

BLOTS: Murderer!

LEDA: Why, I never heard of a . . .

MUDD: *(Interrupting)* Oh, be quiet, Blots. Don't appall!

PAUL: You call, sir?

MUDD: No, my good man . . . appall, not Paul.

PAUL: Oh.

HEDY: Paul, prepare some good hot tea. I'm sure we all can use some.

BLOTS: *(Pointing toward fireplace)* Right now it's sizzling in the fire, poor thing . . . how utterly gruesome.

LEDA: What about your son, Mr. Blots? Did you ever stop to consider how gruesome that is?

BLOTS: It's none of your business.

MOTHER: His son? What about his son? What's he done?

HEDY: Nothing, mother. It's not what his son has done; it's what this vile monster has done!

MOTHER: What?

MUDD: It seems old Blots, here, has left his boy to rot in some god-forsaken place, so he says.

MOTHER: Oh, heavenly days!

Enter Father

FATHER: What's all the rumpus about?

HEDY: Oh, father! I thought you went out?

FATHER: So I did. I pray it's expected of me to return sooner or later.

HEDY: It is. It is. We need you. Mother needs you.

FATHER: Fiddle-faddle! She knows I hate her.

MOTHER: O-o-o-oh! *(Goes into half-faint)*

HEDY: Father, how could you?

FATHER: It's easy daughter; I suggest you oughta, also.

HEDY: Oughta what, father?

FATHER: Hate her like I do. But don't bother.

HEDY: I think you're cruel! And after all mother's been through, too! How could you?

BLOTS: Killing a poor innocent creature.

FATHER: Who is that slobbering lecher?

MUDD: That's Mr. Blots, a lecher, true.

FATHER: *(Sarcastically)* And you?

HEDY: Father!

FATHER: What in the name of St. George are all these people doing in my house?

PEGGY: *(Whispers)* The louse.

HEDY: They're my guests.

MUDD: Sir, my name is Mudd.

FATHER: Well, if your name isn't Mudd!

MUDD: Yes, and I . . .

FATHER: Ha-ha-ha-ha, so your name is Mudd, ha-ha-ha. Tell me, Mudd, when you tell somebody you're going to do something or your name will be Mudd, how—ha-ha-ha, does it strike this somebody, eh? Ha-ha-ha!

MUDD: I'm sorry, sir. I don't quite understand.

FATHER: You don't; you *don't!* Oh-ha-ha-ha-ha-ha.

HEDY: Father, I'll not allow you to insult my guests!

FATHER: Pests! you mean. Get them out of my house! I'll not have . . . *(Paul enters with tea. To Paul)* And just what are you doing?

PAUL: Tea is ready, Miss Hedy.

FATHER: *(To Paul)* "Tea's ready, Miss Hedy," eh? You get your blooming self to the servants quarters and . . .

LEDA: Eeeek!

MUDD: Good Lord! Not another?

HEDY: *(Her mother faints)* Mother!

FATHER: What in God's name is wrong?

PEGGY: This is getting tedious.

FATHER: *(To Leda)* What is it, girl? Come on, give out!

LEDA: There, under the table . . . it's hideous!

FATHER: Ahhhhh! a roach! What's it doing here? Kill it; do something, somebody!

MUDD: Paul, this time you make the approach.

PAUL: Y-y-y-es, sir.

BLOTS: No! This time I'll not permit it! They have already fallen into your brutal hands . . . this one shall not!

FATHER: What? Are you mad, man? It's a roach!

BLOTS: So it is; and so it'll be!

MUDD: Go to it, Paul. I'll stand behind you, I'll coach.

PAUL: Y-y-y-es, sir.

BLOTS: *(Takes sword off wall)* Make one more move, servant, and you're a goner, on my honor!

FATHER: Be sensible, man, we just can't leave it there . . . what if it has friends or worse still, a wife? It's in the law of nature to take its life!

PEGGY: That wouldn't be too wise . . . then a thousand roaches will come to its wake.

LEDA: This is about all I can take. *(Starts to exit)*

BLOTS: No one leaves, until this roach leaves. *(He waves sword at her)* It's an order.

MUDD: Blots . . . try to be reasonable. One roach more or less means nothing, now does it? Especially when it's on the cuff.

BLOTS: That's how that stupid son of mine felt . . . he

wouldn't eat his squash, yet he'd go around squashing roaches easy enough!

FATHER: *(To Hedy, pointing to his wife who is still prostrate on the floor)* Tell that woman to get up from that absurd position.

HEDY: No. Mother has fainted; it's her disposition. Insects cause her blood to rush down to her feet.

FATHER: Her face looks as red as a beet to me.

PEGGY: *(To Blots)* Look, what if it doesn't move? We can be here for days. Why don't you take it out, or better yet, take it home with you?

BLOTS: I'll tell you all something not one of you ever knew: A roach goes where it goes because it must. It would be cruel to take him away;—he's undoubtedly made a long journey to get to this house.

HEDY: But why my house? . . . It's never been sympathetic to bugs, flys, gnats, ants; why, not even a mouse!

BLOTS: I don't know why your house . . . all I know is that a roach goes where it goes.

MUDD: All right, granted. Now suppose that you put that sword away, and we all forget about the roach—*(Turning to the guests)* After all, really, what harm can a mere insignificant roach cause?

LEDA: What harm, you say? Just pause to think awhile . . . Why all the harm in the world, you buffoon! It carries disease and plague, and puts its germs on food and babies and . . .

MUDD: Pooh! You're thinking of worms and that sort. *(He faces Blots)* Now, come, Blots, be a sport, put away the sword.

BLOTS: You promise then not to harm it?

MUDD: We promise, old chap; in fact, we're all somewhat bored. That infernal roach can do what it well pleases to do.

Blots puts sword back on wall. Then Paul immediately runs up to the roach and stamps his foot on it.

BLOTS: You killed it! . . . After you promised you wouldn't . . . scoundrel! Cad!

PAUL: I did it, and I'm glad!

Blots sits down and weeps pathetically. Suddenly there is a great thunder and clash of lightning and rain starts to fall heavily against the windows.

LEDA: It's a storm! The rain's coming down in jugs!

BLOTS: It's the bugs! They're falling from heaven! It's the Revenge of the *Bugs!*

MUDD: *(Looking out the window)* The man's insane . . . it's not raining bugs a-tall . . . it's raining rain.

PEGGY: How will I ever get to my flat?

LEDA: And mine?

MUDD: And mine?

HEDY: It's not as all bad as that. You're all welcomed to

spend the night here.

MOTHER: *(Revived)* What happened?—Oh, is it dead?

PAUL: Utterly, madam.

MOTHER: Thank God.

HEDY: Thank Paul, instead. Was he who killed it.

MOTHER: Thank you; it was thoughtful and sweet of you, Paul.

PAUL: Not a-tall, not a-tall.

FATHER: I'll not have these people sleep in my house, rain or shine!

PEGGY: *(Whispers)* The swine.

BLOTS: It's the bugs . . . they've come to revenge what you have done.

FATHER: Least of all, that one! *(Pointing to Blots)*

MUDD: Blots, have you no pity for your son? He's out there, in all this rain, you know . . . what without clothes and being tied to a tree; Blots, it's the first place where lightning will strike!

BLOTS: The bugs . . . it's raining bugs!

FATHER: The man's definitely pots. I'll phone for the police.

MUDD: That's the fellow!

FATHER: *(Goes to the phone)* Hello . . . hello . . . hello . . . The line is dead. What will we do?

MUDD: We can lock him in a room . . . tie him to a bed.

FATHER: Good idea . . . smart chap; I take back what I said, Mudd. You've got a head on your shoulders.

MUDD: Thank you. I am a book-keeper, by trade. Just recently I was made head-book-keeper for Johnathan Phits & Sons. I was awarded for my exact counts and cleanliness toward my ledgers and folders.

FATHER: Splendid, splendid. Now let's get to it. *(He turns to Paul)* Paul.

PAUL: You call, sir?

FATHER: Yes, I called . . . I want you to dig up some strong twine, good strong stuff, understand?

PAUL: Yes, sir! *(Exits, running)*

FATHER: Mudd, which would you prefer, the legs or the head?

MUDD: The head, sir. It's the legs I dread.

FATHER: Hmmm, yes . . . they kick don't they? Well, Paul is strong enough to handle it.

HEDY: Father, why don't you first find out where his son is?

FATHER: Now why in the name of St. George should I want to find out where his idiot son is?

LEDA: Mr. Mudd, you ask him.

MUDD: Blots . . . where is your son?

BLOTS: Not one, not two, nor three, nor four, or five! but a million! bugs shall rain upon this house, and shall crumple it till none is left alive!

Enter Paul

PAUL: Sir, there's no twine to be found.

FATHER: Boot it! He need not be bound. We'll lock him in securely.

MUDD: But surely, it would be wiser to bind him.

FATHER: Right you are, Mudd. We'll do it with sheets.

BLOTS: They'll come in hordes . . . in fleets!

LEDA: Oh, no!

HEDY: Leda, don't mind him.

BLOTS: They'll be millions and millions and they'll come with the heeby-jeebys and fire!

LEDA: I'm frightened!

FATHER: Paul, get some sheets . . . better still, some wire!

LEDA: Tell him to stop! He's driving me mad the way he groans!

BLOTS: They'll come and they'll eat your eyes and they'll drink your blood and they'll brood their young on your bones!

LEDA: O-o-o-o-oh!

Enter Paul, with wire

PAUL: The wire, sir.

FATHER: *(Takes it from Paul and gives it to Mudd)* Here, Mudd. Tie sturdy knots.

MUDD: *(Walks cautiously toward Blots)* All right, Blots. Easy now . . . easy . . . easy . . .

Paul and the father grab Blots; he struggles. Mudd ties him up and they take him off stage.

HEDY: Whew! I'm glad that's done with.

PEGGY: It's raining harder and harder. The poor boy out there . . . I only hope it's a myth.

LEDA: It could well be . . . that man's definitely off his rocker.

HEDY: I do hope it ceases to rain. Mr. Mudd intends to escort me to a game of soccer.

MOTHER: Put on the radio . . . let's get the news.

Hedy turns on radio

RADIO: Now for an hour of solemn blues . . . wait! here's a bulletin just in. Felonious Bligh has just escaped from Honestview Prison. Be on the lookout! Here is his description: a five inch scar on the left side of his neck, brown hair, blue eyes, aquiline nose. He's 170 lbs; 5 ft 10 inches.

This man is dangerous, and he may be armed! He is a professed hater of mankind! When Judge Sweets sentenced him to 80 years in prison, his last words were *I hate mankind!* So ladies and gentlemen, be on the lookout. Lock all your doors, all your windows; keep one window clear so that you can be on the lookout! Don't under any circumstances let any one in your house! It could well be . . . Felonious Bligh!

MOTHER: Oh, my! Hedy, quick, lock the door before he gets here!

PEGGY: Now, dear, Honestview is as far from here as the dusk is to the dawn.

LEDA: But you heard what the radio said; it said lock the door, the windows!

HEDY: Don't excite yourselves . . . I've already locked those.

Enter Paul, Mudd, Father

MUDD: Well, no longer fear, ladies . . . the situation is well in hand.

PAUL: The menace has thus been abolished!

LEDA: How wonderfully grand!

MOTHER: *(Examining lamps)* Paul, these lamps . . . they've not been polished today.

PAUL: Forgive me, madam, I've been so busy—what with all this horror, and that man's depraved abuse.

MOTHER: That's no excuse!

FATHER: Shut up, woman, before I . . .

LEDA: Have you heard? Felonious Bligh has absconded prison!

MUDD:
FATHER: Felonious Bligh!
PAUL:

PEGGY: We're all to be on the lookout, the radio said.

HEDY: He's armed . . . he's got a gun!

LEDA: The radio said he hates everyone!

MOTHER: He'll shoot us dead!

FATHER: Paul, make certain every door, every window in the entire house is securely locked.

PAUL: Yes, sir. *(He goes about the room examining windows)*

FATHER: Hedy, get me my pistol.

HEDY: Father, it's still hocked.

FATHER: By George, so it is. Oh, well, don't bother. That sword'll do the trick.

MUDD: Sir, there's really no cause for alarm. The infidel would hardly pick this estate.

LEDA: How can you tell?

PEGGY: It's fairly obvious, there's a thousand homes between here and Honestview.

FATHER: True. Still I'd like to take every precaution.

MOTHER: Felonious Bligh . . . was it he that gave Lady Dorchester her abortion?

PEGGY: 'Twas he.

MOTHER: Oh, the abominable hoodlum!

FATHER: Should someone knock on the door, leave it to me; I shall answer it.

LEDA: And it was he that a Russian dancer hit. He offered to kiss her foot, knowing full well that that was where she hid her loot!

HEDY: He always lurks in distinguished society.

PAUL: Hurumph! . . . the confounded impropriety.

MUDD: I say, this storm is really kicking up.

PEGGY: Seems more like a hurricane to me.

PAUL: Sir, the rain . . . it's leaking through the ceiling!

FATHER: Get a cup, put it under it.

LEDA: *(Pointing up at the ceiling)* Look, the paint, it's peeling!

FATHER: Turn on the radio; see what it's got to say.

Hedy turns on the radio

RADIO: He is dangerous, and is certain to be armed. Remember, be on the lookout! Now for the other side of the news. Parson Beanbelly, like a good soldier, went down with his church today, in the year's worst storm. The South Church was more than 200 years old. Thus another landmark disembarks. Farewell, South Church! We grieve thy loss, and farewell, Parson Beanbelly, a true major! Now let us return to our featured program: Grayson at the Jazz Station.

Hedy turns off radio

PEGGY: So, Grayson is still at the Jazz Station.

MUDD: Why, Miss Sax, I didn't know you dug jazz?

PEGGY: Didn't you? I thought every one knew. No one told you?

MUDD: No one has. Pity.

PEGGY: Yes, I guess we could have enjoyed many a session together.

LEDA: *(Looking out of window)* Darn this weather!

Enter Paul with plate of tarts

PAUL: *(To mother)* Tarts, madam?

MOTHER: Splendid. I didn't know we had them. *(She ventures to eat a whole one)*

HEDY: Mother, break it into parts, or you'll choke on it.

MOTHER: Nonsense. It's a mere morsel.

HEDY: Father, mother eats like an athlete.

FATHER: She eats like a horse will.

HEDY: Father! Be discrete.

The mother begins to choke. She stands up, grabs her throat, and is speechless. She goes into a fit of spasms, falls to the floor, and dies.

HEDY: Mother! *(Rushes across the room, kneels beside her mother and gives a scream)* Mother!

FATHER: By George, what has happened?

MUDD: Has she fainted again?

PEGGY: I don't know . . . think she saw another insect?

MUDD: There doesn't seem to be any in sight, but I'll inspect.

LEDA: She choked on the tart!

HEDY: Father, feel her heart.

FATHER: *(Feeling heart)* It's . . . it's stopped beating!

HEDY: *(Hugging her mother)* No no!

MUDD: What did you say she was eating?

LEDA: A tart . . . a blueberry tart.

MUDD: All of it, or just a part?

HEDY: All of it . . . all of it. *(Sobbing)*

MUDD: How awful!

PAUL: The madam had her jaw full, then she swallowed . . . well, you know what followed.

FATHER: She choked to death!

LEDA: She is dead.

PEGGY: True, she was fighting to regain her breath.

PAUL: But she died instead.

MUDD: Look! Did her eye just wink?

HEDY: Did it? Did it? . . . Oh, I can't think!

PAUL: No, 'twas only rigor mortis setting in.

FATHER: *(Picking up a tart from the dish)* Who brought this?

PAUL: I did, sir; madam requested it.

FATHER: Strange . . . I always thought she detested sweets . . .

HEDY: No, not sweets; she loved sweets. She hated pickles, olives, beets. But how would you know, you hated her!

MUDD: Sir, after examining this tart I find it to be poisoned; your wife has been assassinated!

LEDA: She didn't choke then?

FATHER: Mudd, are you certain?

MUDD: Sir, I have spoken!

FATHER: I'm fascinated!

LEDA: Who would do such a thing? Mr. Mudd, would you know?

MUDD: Yes, most likely a foe!

LEDA: Could . . . it . . . have . . . been . . . Blots!

There is a pause; they eye each other questioningly, suspiciously.

PEGGY: Blots?

LEDA: Yes.

FATHER: Hmmmmm.

MUDD: Ah-ha!

PAUL: There's no other suspect!

PEGGY: Except . . .

FATHER: Yes?

They all eye her suspiciously.

PEGGY: Except, Felonious Bligh!

MUDD: Nonsense. Felonious Bligh is not a murderer. In fact he considers it quite parsimonious.

FATHER: Mudd's right; although I shan't go along with him on Bligh not being a murderer. Bligh couldn't have done it. What cause would he have? Where's the motive?

PEGGY: Ha-ha! There's the rub. There is no motive to this murder. That is why I name Felonious Bligh number one suspect. Bligh is noted to hate mankind . . . therefore he'll kill without motive. Really, it's an open and shut case.

PAUL: How utterly base!

MUDD: I can't accept your theory. Felonious Bligh escaped not more than an hour ago; Honestview is a good 30 kilometers from here; it would be impossible for him to have come this far in so short a time. And why, pray do tell me, if he did come this far would he poison blueberry tarts? It's too absurd! I'm sorry, Miss Peggy Sax, your theory is not at all harmonious with the facts.

FATHER: Mudd, do you think it was Blots?

MUDD: I'm not certain . . . there are some spots yet to be analyzed in this case.

FATHER: If I find out it was him I'll have him swinging in space!

PEGGY: If there has been foul play we should call the police at once!

FATHER: The phone is dead.

MUDD: I say we should question Blots ourselves instead of the police.

FATHER: Right, Mudd. You shall be prosecutor, and I shall be the Justice of the Peace. Ladies, you shall be the jury; and Paul, I elect you to be the counsel for the accused.

PAUL: *(Rubbing hands, grinning)* With pleasure, sir. I am most enthused!

FATHER: We shall be fair and shall give him his due measure.

HEDY: That vile creature killed my mother!

FATHER: Steady, girl. I can always marry another.

LEDA: I say we get on with the case!

PEGGY: I say we first gather all the facts.

MUDD: True, Miss Sax. *(Turns to Paul)* Paul, get all the data you can for your client and present it at the trial. What evidence I have, I too, will present at the trial.

FATHER: Let us go then and fetch him. Paul, Mudd, come.

They exit.

PEGGY: *(Picks up phone . . . pause)* True, there is no dial tone.

LEDA: So, you stand alone . . . you don't want the trial!

PEGGY: I'm still convinced it was Bligh.

LEDA: Well, not I.

HEDY: Nor I.

PEGGY: *(Looking out window)* I've never seen it rain so!

HEDY: *(Kneeling by her mother)* Her eyes . . . such a calm plain glow.

LEDA: Hedy, put a lily in her hand.

HEDY: No.

LEDA: It's silly, I understand. But it is the usual formality.

HEDY: She was a great woman.

LEDA: True, a woman of fine morality.

HEDY: But she's dead.

LEDA: No. Say she's sleeping, instead.

HEDY: Yes, that's it, she sleeps.

LEDA: And think of her in dreamland in a beautiful garden where little birds cheep and chirp.

HEDY: Yes. Yes. I can almost hear the cheeps; the chirps . . .

Enter Mudd, Paul and the father with Blots. They tie him to a chair, and then proceed to set the room up as a court room.

FATHER: Let the trial begin. *(He strikes desk with hammer.)* Counsel for the defendant will swear the culprit in.

PAUL: *(Holding book in hand, puts Blots hand on it)* Do you solemnly swear to tell the truth the whole truth and nothing but the truth?

BLOTS: Bugs!

MUDD: Your Honor, I object. What book is that the client's attorney has in his hand? I state it is not a Bible. I further state that the attorney is in cahoots with the culprit!

PAUL: *(Confused)* But, sir! I . . .

FATHER: Attorney, let me see the book! *(Paul hands him the book.) Tropic of Cancer,* why this is blasphemy!

PAUL: *(More confused)* I just picked it at random, sir. *(He points to bookshelf)* There, the bookshelf . . .

FATHER: From here on in watch yourself, Attorney, or you'll be liable for contempt! Now get a Bible.

Paul scratches his head, goes to shelf and looks.

PAUL: Sir, there isn't any Bible!

FATHER: By George! All right bring over *Death in the Afternoon. (He looks across to Mudd.)* Good as any. I've always been impressed with it.

Paul returns with the book and proceeds

PAUL: Do you solemnly swear to tell the truth the whole truth and nothing but the truth?

BLOTS: The bugs are coming!

FATHER: All right, Prosecutor, proceed to prosecute.

MUDD: Blots, is your sickness acute?

No answer

MUDD: Well, answer me!

No answer

MUDD: *(To the father)* Sir, the defendant will not answer. Therefore, it is fairly obvious that he is concealing something.

FATHER: Blots, what are you concealing?

BLOTS: They shall seek their revenge!

MUDD: Revenge! Ah, so you admit you wanted revenge?

No answer

MUDD: Blots, do you or don't you admit it?

No answer

MUDD: Your honor, surely it is evident that the accused is lying. A great sign of guilt it is when a defendant is silent. He has refused to answer, It proves thus that he will not talk. It further proves the knife is not of any use without the fork!

PAUL: Your honor, I don't quite understand that last sentence.

FATHER: Objection overruled. Continue, Prosecutor.

MUDD: Blots, you live in London, don't you? You are a commuter, are you not?

BLOTS: They'll kill!

MUDD: Kill! Did you say, kill? *(Pause)* Your Honor, need I continue? The man has admitted his guilt. *(He turns to jury)* Kind jury, judge as thou wilt. But *(He flashes forth a hankie and puts it to his eyes.)* but this I must say to you before that counselor, that Atheist who desecrated our Lord's Bible, cross-examined the culprit. I must say that I think all children sweet little things, and all mothers courageous proud images of God. I believe that women should have equal rights because they bear the burden of children and of housekeeping.

Ladies, I never had a mother. *(He sobs.)* She passed away when I was a tiny tot. But did that shatter me!? Not! I still have faith in womanhood! I still admire!

I know there is something higher up there *(Points*

to ceiling) yet I still praise the splendid courage of all women! My mother . . . *(Sniffles)* she was just another woman. But *not* just another woman! She fought the bitter claws of famine; the insidious jaws of winter! She sold matches, toothpicks, garlic . . . everything, until one day she became sick. Ladies, although I was a tot, I took care of her. I cheated, I lied, but I took care of her! *(Weeps)* Yet no use. She died.

Hedy and Leda and the father break down weeping

FATHER: *(Sobbing)* Do you rest your case, sad Prosecutor?

MUDD: I do.

FATHER: *(Angrily)* All right, Counselor, defend your client!

PAUL: *(Shakened)* Yes, sir. *(He goes up to Blots.)* Mr. Blots, tell the jury why you are silent. Is it because you are vile?

BLOTS: I can hear the prattle of tiny feet. They're coming, coming.

PAUL: What feet? Whose feet?

MUDD: Your Honor, I object! We all know he means the feet of an insect.

FATHER: Objection sustained. Mr. Counselor, from here on in please refrain from being repetitious.

PAUL: Yes, sir. *(Back to Blots)* Mr. Blots, is it true that you associate with people slightly meretritious?

No answer

PAUL: Mr. Blots, are you or are you not a menace?

BLOTS: You murderer! you killed that poor innocent creature!

FATHER: What is this allegation?

PAUL: Sir, mere instigation. I rest my case.

FATHER: Very well, you may appeal to the jury.

PAUL: Thank you, sir. *(To the jury)* Ladies, I feel that one of the greatest of man's qualities is the respect of his fellow man. I have always respected my fellow man. When he wants his tea, I am there to bring it to him. If he wants his tea iced, he gets its iced. If he wants it otherwise, he gets it otherwise. But this defendant! He has not the least respect for his fellow man. He accuses me with his horrid animosity. But, ladies of the jury, my kind generosity forgives him.

MUDD: Your Honor, the counsel for defense is being innately cynical.

FATHER: Counselor, watch yourself!

PAUL: Yes, sir. *(Back to jury)* Has ever such a fiend *(Pointing to Blots)* reached such a pinnacle! Ladies, consider that and be merciful. That is all.

FATHER: The Jury will confer.

The ladies confer. Leda then stands.

FATHER: Have you reached a verdict?

LEDA: Yes, your Honor, we have.

FATHER: *(Whispering to Mudd)* Mudd, what do you predict?

MUDD: Guilty.

FATHER: So do I. *(To Leda)* What is your verdict?

LEDA: Hedy and I say, guilty! Peggy says Felonious Bligh.

FATHER: That does it. *(Brings down hammer)* Two to one!

PAUL: *(Going over too Mudd, shaking his hand)* Sir, congratulations, well done.

MUDD: *(Philosophically)* The forbidden fruit is quickly turned to ash!

PEGGY: *(To the father)* Sir, will the penalty be in the form of a lash?

FATHER: *(Ignoring her)* Blots, do you have anything to say before I impose judgment upon you?

BLOTS: Bugs!

FATHER: I hereby decree that you die by a blueberry tart! May the Lord have mercy on your soul. Case closed! Paul, you shall serve as executioner. Go fetch a tart and execute, now!

PEGGY: This I'll not allow!

FATHER: He had a fair trial.

PEGGY: But can't you wait awhile? The phone will soon be back in order.

FATHER: We can't afford a new trial. As it stands justice has been fairly executed . . . no one else has refuted. The accused was silent; who ever is silent, conceals. Ergo, let the sentence be enforced. His Counsel has refused the Court of Appeals.

PAUL: Sir, as executioner, is it my duty to hand the condemned a tart?

FATHER: Yes, but if the condemned refuses to eat it, then it is your job to force it down his throat.

PEGGY: Sir, please let us be conciliated.

FATHER: Not in the least.

LEDA: The crime must be expiated.

PEGGY: But what about a priest?

HEDY: The man is an infidel.

PAUL: Quite, plus he's pertinently insolent.

PEGGY: But his soul might burn in Hell! Please, sir, consider, in Hell a man's thirst is never satiated!

FATHER: Plain hearsay.

LEDA: The crime must be expiated.

MUDD: True, 'tis the will of God.

PAUL: I dare say.

PEGGY: *(Raging)* I wash my hands of this madness! I am no part of this insanity!

HEDY: She calls us insane, yet outside all it ever does is rain! *(Cries)*

FATHER: Executioner, administer the tart!

Paul hands the tart to Blots. Blots eats the tart hungrily. He goes into a fit. Dies.

There is a knock on the door. The father goes to the door.

FATHER: Who is it?

VOICE: A friend.

FATHER: What cause you visit?

VOICE: Relief from the storm. I seek refuge.

FATHER: Sorry, not here.

VOICE: But, kind sir, there's a deluge!

HEDY: Oh, dear!—father, let him in.

Father opens the door slowly. Suddenly the voice enters, throwing door wide open.

VOICE: 'Tis I, Felonious Bligh!

EVERYONE: Felonious Bligh?

BLIGH: *(Comes in and sits down, making himself comfortable)* Ah, fear not! In this world of glee I would humbly supplicate thee. 'Tis not me fashion to be rude, I just want all ye got in way of food.

PAUL: Perhaps a tart, sir?

BLIGH: Have ye any meats?

PAUL: Sorry, sir, just tarts and maple sweets.

BLIGH: *(Noticing the two bodies)* What's wrong with those two?

MUDD: They're resting, Sir Bligh.

BLIGH: With their clothes on?

MUDD: It's their custom, Sir Bligh.

BLIGH: Me name's Felonious, I ain't been knighted yet.

MUDD: Pardon. I'd be delighted to call you Felonious, sir.

BLIGH: Saw a strange sight a couple a miles from here. Some poor lad naked . . . tied to a tree he was.

LEDA: Where?

BLIGH: Forgot the spot, mam.

HEDY: It must be Blots' son!

PAUL: *(Offering Bligh a tart)* Here you are, Mr. Bligh.

BLIGH: *(Taking it and eating it)* Much obliged. *(Bligh dies.)*

MUDD: Paul, you'll get a reward for this!

FATHER: A hero! And in our household, too!

LEDA: Quick! Call the police. We caught Felonious Bligh!

HEDY: How mother would have loved this! if only she didn't die.

FATHER: I'm mighty proud of you, Paul.

PAUL: It comes in the line of duty, sure. I am above all your servant.

FATHER: Well put, well put.

PAUL: I shall always be by to answer any call.

FATHER: All right, let's not get corny, Paul.

HEDY: *(Trying phone)* The phone's working!

LEDA: Really, Paul, such quick thinking on your part.

MUDD: *(Going to phone)* I'll call Scotland Yard.

PAUL: Nothing to it. He said he was hungry, so I gave him a tart.

PEGGY: How many tarts are left?

PAUL: Two.

PEGGY: Well, those you had better discard.

PAUL: True. *(He exits with tarts.)*

MUDD: *(Into phone)* Hello, Scotland Yard?

LEDA: Look, it's stopped raining!

HEDY: Yes, so it has.

MUDD: This is Mr. Mudd. We've captured Felonious Bligh!

PEGGY: Hedy, I really had a delightful evening. Although, I must say I wasn't too happy about the verdict.

MUDD: Yes, Felonious Bligh!

PEGGY: But who could really depict things of that sort? Do drop over to my place for tea in the near future.

HEDY: I shall.

MUDD: He's here. On the floor! Bligh, on the floor; he's here.

PEGGY: Goodbye, everyone.

LEDA: Goodbye.

FATHER: Goodbye.

MUDD: *(Looking up from phone)* Bye, Miss Sax. See you at Grayson's! *(Back into the phone)* Let me speak to the Inspector.

Peggy exits.

LEDA: *(To Hedy)* Did you see the dress she wore? I doubt if she has another one. It's the fifth time I've seen her wear it.

HEDY: But, my deah, that wasn't what shocked me! Did you take notice of her shoes?

LEDA: Yes, later.

HEDY: Imitation alligator!

MUDD: Hello, Inspector? This is Mr. Mudd. Mudd, M-u-d-d. Yes. Well, we've got Bligh.

FATHER: Paul!

Enter Paul, hurriedly and nervously

PAUL: Yes, sir.

FATHER: What took you so long getting here?

PAUL: Sorry, sir.

FATHER: Prepare supper.

PAUL: Yes, sir. *(He exits.)*

MUDD: *(Hangs up phone)* Sir, the Inspector said amazing; he congratulated you. He sounded well pleased.

FATHER: *(Seemingly proud)* Yes, I'm sure he is somewhat eased. These are the times that try men's souls.

MUDD: Yes. Well, I must be getting on, sir.

HEDY: Aren't you going to stay for dinner?

MUDD: It's terribly kind of you, Miss Hedy. But I did have some of your tea, and a few of your nuts. I wouldn't want to exercise your hospitality.

FATHER: Nonsense, Mudd. Stay for supper.

MUDD: Impossible, sir. I must leave.

FATHER: If you must, you must. Remember keep a stiff upper . . .

MUDD: I shall remember, sir.

HEDY: Goodbye, Mr. Mudd. You were the life of the party.

LEDA: Yes. You were so enjoyable.

MUDD: Thank you. *(Opens door, goes halfway out; waves back)* Eat well and hardy. *(He exits)*

FATHER: Good chap.

HEDY: Yes. Pity.

LEDA: Can I stay for supper?

Enter Paul

PAUL: Sir, I gather that supper is to be served in the kitchen?

FATHER: Yes.

Exit Paul

LEDA: I think I would like to eat something.

There's a knock on the door. The father opens it. Enter Inspector.

FATHER: Ah, Inspector!

INSPECTOR: Where's Bligh?

FATHER: *(Points to Bligh)* There.

INSPECTOR: It's him, all right. Good work, sir.

FATHER: 'Twas no work a-tall.

INSPECTOR: You have a lady-bug on your shoulder, sir.

FATHER: By George, so I have.

INSPECTOR: Here, permit me, sir. *(He flicks it off.)*

FATHER: Thank you, Inspector.

Enter Paul with tray of tarts

PAUL: Tarts, anyone?

FATHER: No! Get back in the kitchen!

Exit Paul

INSPECTOR: I would have loved a tart, sir.

FATHER: Some other time.

INSPECTOR: As you like. They're your tarts.

END

Standing on a Streetcorner

A Little Play (1953)

The time is today and the place is 12th Street & 6th Ave. and the hero is a happy doltish chubby young man who spends most of his time observing people and things. Today he is observing the corner of 12th Street & 6th Ave. He watches a march of housewives and children who carry signs like NO SHELTERS—MORE SCHOOLS; NO BOMBS—MORE ALMS. He does all he can to keep from getting swept into the march—he hugs the lamppost; the march passes him; at the end of it are two fat ladies carrying big fat signs; he talks to them.

YOUNG MAN: Hey do you know what I think I think fallout shelters ain't so bad, I mean what they stand for is awful but consider this: a nice family owns one, and one day that father, all tired from work, wants some privacy, peace, *solitude*—so he gets up from the dinner table and says to his wife and sons and daughters "I'm gonna go fall out in the fallout shelter." You see? It can be put to good use! For privacy! Sometimes people have got to be alone, so if they have fallout shelters they can be alone. Just leave the dinner table and take a nice book along and close the shelter door, turn on the air conditioner, and lie down comfortably and read!

1ST FAT LADY: I'll die before I put my kids in one of them!

2ND FAT LADY: Young man, I have a young daughter—would you like your young daughter to sit in one of them concrete tombs.

YOUNG MAN: Gee, I wish I had a young daughter—you're right, of course, and that's why I'm talking to you because I know you're all right and—well, if I had a young daughter then maybe she'd like the shelter because what if she wanted to kiss her boy friend, what a wonderful place for a love nest! See? I mean, what harm can an extra room do? If the bomb falls then of course it's bad, but I don't think the bomb's gonna fall so watch and see: all them fallout shelters are going to end up being meditation rooms, love nests, and the such—you watch!

1ST FAT LADY: Ah, this one's a dreamer—he should know, he should only know!

2ND FAT LADY: Action, not talk! Not dreams! Action is needed! And we are marching!

They march away. A little girl walks up to Young Man and stands beside him.

YOUNG MAN: Ah, you wish me to help you cross the street, my fair little maiden? O.K. Here, take my hand and I'll cross you. There, the light's red.

LADY: *(Running up to them and grabbing the little girl away)* What do you think you are doing! She's my baby!

YOUNG MAN: Oh, I'm sorry lady but I thought she wanted me to help her cross the street—

LADY: *(Looking him up and down suspiciously—she scolds the child.)* Don't you ever do that again!

YOUNG MAN: God what did she think I was a monster or something, all I wanted to do was help, but I guess people have got to be very careful today because who knows what can happen, in fact anything can happen, and often does.

He suddenly starts clapping his hands wildly at two men who dashed from the other side of the street to his side—sidestepping the oncoming traffic.

YOUNG MAN: Hurray! You guys made it! It was green light, you know.

The two men give him a he's-nuts look and move on.

YOUNG MAN: They don't realize how commendable they are crossing a green light like that—6th Avenue is a fast street and the cars go fast and you got to be awfully fast not to get hit or something. It's like facing the bull almost.

OLD LADY: *(She is bent and old in black wear with cane. Young Man gleefully takes her by the arm and ventures to lead her across the street.)* Help! Leave me alone!

YOUNG MAN: I only want to help you cross the street—

OLD LADY: But I don't wish to cross!

YOUNG MAN: You don't want to? I thought you wanted to—I'm sorry—

And the Old Lady walks the other way. A policeman passes by and from the corner of his eye looks the Young Man up and down and slowly moves on. A man with a covered bird cage stops by the Young Man waiting for the light.

YOUNG MAN: Ooooh, can I see!

MAN: It's sleeping.

YOUNG MAN: What kind of bird is it?

MAN: Owl.

YOUNG MAN: I love owls! I really do! They're my favorite bird! Please let me peek?

MAN: *(He pulls aside covering.)* It's awake.

YOUNG MAN: I'm sorry, but I do love owls, and when have I last seen an owl! *(He puts his finger in cage.)* Here owl owl, here owl—

MAN: It bites.

YOUNG MAN: They're the most beautiful of birds—

MAN: I gotta go.

YOUNG MAN: It's green light. What are you going to do with it—what's its name? *(Light turns red. Man crosses street.)* Hey, where can I get one?

MAN: Pet shop.

YOUNG MAN: Thank you very much, sir!

The policeman returns and stands a few feet away watching the Young Man with deep suspicion.

POLICEMAN: Hey, you waiting for somebody?

YOUNG MAN: No, Officer, I'm just standing.

POLICEMAN: Just standing? What for?

YOUNG MAN: I'm not doing anything wrong officer.

POLICEMAN: Don't you got anything better to do? *(He walks away shaking his head as it to say there-are-some-kind-of-people-in-this-world.)*

YOUNG MAN: *(Watching the policeman walk away)* And what about you, haven't you anything better to do? I know why, because I'm doing what he's doing, just hanging around; and it makes him uncomfortable. For him people mustn't do what he's doing. That's how it was in that museum. Boy, did I learn a thing or two there! I went in, leaving the street all natural and such, and wham! I find myself looking at pictures. That's what museums do, they hook people, get them on the museum beam. Well, I went in not to look at the pictures like all the others but leaned against the wall looking at what the guard was looking at. Was it mandatory that I look at the pictures? Besides, I think it's kind of spooky to come off the street all natural and everything and then wham move my eyes from picture to picture. I walked through that museum as naturally as walking down a street. I wasn't gonna get hooked, no sir. Something funny about museum people, all over the world, they're the same, just like subway people, all alike. I don't mind being like them but does that mean I have to be like them all the time?

PRETTY LADY: Could you please tell me where the New School is please?

YOUNG MAN: *(Moved by her beauty)* What are you studying?

PRETTY LADY: Please, I'm quite pressed for time.

YOUNG MAN: It's right over there—but I don't think it's a very good school because once I paid thirty dollars for a music appreciation course and only went to the first class and no more. I paid to hear the teacher not the people in the class. The teacher played Bach's Mass in B Minor and everybody, mostly long-black-haired girls, to show how smart and musical they were, went "ooooooh, ahhhhh, Bach, it's Bach" when they shoulda kept quiet and their emotions to themselves, don't you agree?

The Pretty Lady is gone. A Lady crosses the street with the light green—again the Young Man applauds loudly.

LADY: Why for you clap like that?

YOUNG MAN: Because what you did was like fighting a bull!

LADY: What? Where you come from Bellevue or something? Fight what bull?

And away she trudges.

YOUNG MAN: *(Running after her)* Yes, you see, by crossing the street with all the cars coming at you like that, which is very dangerous and daring on your part, I clapped in admiration for you because you took as much a chance doing that as does a bullfighter, do you see?

LADY: You crazy! Everybody today crazy! It's the bomb, it's Khrushchev, he do this to us, make us nuts! Go home, be good, go home—

YOUNG MAN: *(Returns to his corner and leans against the mailbox and looks up at the sky, remains like that for quite some time and then exclaims:)* Long live the sky! Up and always up is the sky! *(Suddenly he smacks his face.)* Hey wait a minute! Wait a minute! Not always up is the sky but down too is the sky! Yes! because if the earth is round like they say and not attached to anything then that means the

sky is underneath the earth too! So down too is the sky! Boy what a discovery! How nice it is that I'm always discovering things, just by doing nothing! Like the time I discovered about America being the new promised land like ancient Israel was. I figured that there was no difference between Christ and Christopher Columbus because Christ was born of Saint Mary and Christopher, who has almost the same first name, was born of the Santa Maria, and also they died sadly too, so I figured that America must be the new promised land and all that—

A hurrying man stops by for light.

YOUNG MAN: Sir, don't you think America is like ancient Israel because when the flood came they had Noah's ark, and today when the bomb falls they'll have fallout shelters—but it won't be the same, no sir, no two aardvarks, no two ducks, two owls, and all that, but goopy creepy families with elephant guns so that nobody take refuge with them. So it isn't all the same really because the American flood don't seem God-inspired at all—

The man long since has hurried across the street.

POLICEMAN: *(Coming out of nowhere)* All right, now, all right, I've been watching you—what are you asking people for, money? I saw you talk to them—now get a move on!

YOUNG MAN: *(He takes out his wallet and shows the officer six twenty-dollar bills.)* I swear I wasn't asking for no money, officer, honest. Look—see, I don't need money; all I'm doing is watching what's happening—I do it all the time. Yesterday I stood on 22nd and 7th and I didn't bother nobody.

POLICEMAN: Where do you live?

YOUNG MAN: In Brooklyn. Oh, be careful, officer, you have an eyelash near your eye and if it gets in your eye it can be real painful, here let me—

POLICEMAN: No—I'll do it myself.

Policeman wipes his eye.

YOUNG MAN: It's still there.

The Young Man waves good-by to the policeman and enters a barber shop. He sits down.

YOUNG MAN: Shave please.

BARBER: You need a haircut.

YOUNG MAN: I don't need a haircut, I need a shave.

BARBER: If you think you don't need a haircut then you don't need a shave.

YOUNG MAN: I need my hair.

The Barber, a little roughly, lets down the chair and proceeds to shave the Young Man.

BARBER: *(Having finished)* Shampoo?

YOUNG MAN: No thank you.

BARBER: Massage?

YOUNG MAN: No thank you—say, do you think the bomb's gonna fall?

BARBER: The shave is 85 cents.

YOUNG MAN: *(Handing barber twenty-dollar bill)* I don't think it's going to fall, and you know why? Because its too easy to think it'll fall. What's really strange and difficult to imagine is it NEVER falling!

BARBER: *(Handing him change)* Too much thinking about the bomb seems to me like the bomb is doing its damage without having to fall—here's your change.

YOUNG MAN: Right you are! *(He gives Barber big tip.)* What with everybody so bomb conscious it is as though it has fallen in a way, mentally that is, because now they got these shelters and they're always gonna have them and that means that all the babies to come will have to ask what the shelters are, and the parents will have to explain to them, and not many parents can explain death, so the poor kids will have to consult their deaths when everything about them is life. Don't you agree?

BARBER: Sure.

The Young Man leaves the barber shop and walks out and stands on the corner which is near the girls' school and soon the girls will be leaving school and he likes very much to watch them—in fact today he is detemined to seek out a very beautiful girl and talk with her.

A panhandler drunkenly asks him for money.

YOUNG MAN: *(Handing panhandler money)* Say, what do you think about fallout shelters?

PANHANDLER: Say, Mac, dat's orrrfully gooda ya—

YOUNG MAN: Ain't you ever heard of fallout shelters?

PANHANDLER: Give a guy a cigarette, willya?

YOUNG MAN: I don't smoke—but listen, I'll give you another quarter you tell me what you think about the bomb, all right?

PANHANDLER: Boy, buddy, yourrrrr a good buddy.

YOUNG MAN: Here's the quarter, now tell me—

PANHANDLER: Give a guy a cigarette, ol buddy—

YOUNG MAN: *(Moving away from drunken panhandler, and out come the school girls.)* Oh, that's a pretty one! Yes,

I'll talk to her, let me see, what should I say, what should I—Er, miss, can you please tell me where the New School is?

GIRL: I think it's near 13th Street near 6th Avenue.

YOUNG MAN: Up there?

He points uptown.

GIRL: Yes.

YOUNG MAN: Hey, do you know what I discovered only a while ago, would you like to know?

GIRL: I'm in a hurry.

YOUNG MAN: It won't take long to tell.

GIRL: All right, but hurry.

YOUNG MAN: I discovered that the sky is not only up there but down beneath us too!

GIRL: Hell is beneath us.

YOUNG MAN: You believe in hell?

GIRL: Of course, don't you?

YOUNG MAN: I don't know. But scientifically speaking, the sky is all around us, which means we're actually floating in the sky, it's true!

GIRL: And how did you discover that? You an astronaut or something?

YOUNG MAN: Oh no, I just thought it, just like that!

GIRL: I don't think that's such a new discovery—I think somebody else discovered it before you—

YOUNG MAN: Maybe, yes, but where myself is concerned I discovered it for myself, like that other person before me did, you see?

GIRL: Well, good-by.

YOUNG MAN: You're very pretty.

And away flies the young girl like a proud bird. Another pretty girl, a Negro, catches his fancy.

YOUNG MAN: Miss, do your parents have a fallout shelter?

PRETTY NEGRO: They're talking about it. But we live in an apartment, so where we gonna put it? That's what my father said: "Where we gonna put it?!" My mother didn't know, my uncle didn't know; I said maybe the cellar, but my father he said he wasn't prepared to dig a hole in the cellar nohow. Why you asking for?

Young Man: Because that seems to be the question today, to build or not to build.

Pretty Negro: If we had a place to build it in maybe then we'd build it.

Young Man: You don't believe the bomb's gonna fall do you?

Pretty Negro: The papers say like it might.

Young Man: But can you really imagine it falling?

Pretty Negro: How am I supposed to know?

Young Man: I don't know, I thought maybe you might know—

Pretty Negro: I don't know, all I know is it fell before so I don't see why it can't fall again.

Young Man: Hey you're right! I didn't think about that—it's not as if it never fell before, it *did* fall before! The way people sound today is as if it never fell, but it did fall! It did! And that's what makes it so real and sad and horrible, yes! Because if it never fell then maybe everything would be all right—boy, I think you're a very smart girl for showing me that, and you're pretty too—

Pretty Negro: Well, thank you, now I must be going because my mother has my lunch ready—goodie bye!

Young Man: Good-by! Good-by!

He walks around in little circles shaking his head and smiling happily because she was so smart and nice and pretty.

YOUNG MAN: I shoulda asked for her phone number or something. Here comes another pretty girl. Hello, miss, could you—

The girl pays him no notice. He waves good-by to her. Out of nowhere appears a tall impressive-looking man. He approaches the Young Man.

TALL MAN: Perhaps you frightened her.

YOUNG MAN: I guess it's possible that I scare some people because some people scare me. Maybe it was my hair, but why should hair scare people?

TALL MAN: It seldom does.

YOUNG MAN: I got little stars and angels in my hair, that's why I don't get it cut.

TALL MAN: *(Disbelievingly)* How old are you?

YOUNG MAN: Twenty-five.

TALL MAN: I overheard what you said in the barber shop. Did you intend to tell that girl what you told the barber?

YOUNG MAN: *(Slightly perplexed)* I don't know.

TALL MAN: *(Convinced with disbelief)* Can you look me straight in the eye and contend your hair is adorned with little stars and angels?

YOUNG MAN: *(Feeling his hair)* They're not there anymore. I must be unhappy, because when I'm happy they're there —why should I lie? I don't lie.

TALL MAN: *(Contemptuously)* You lied to that barber, my friend.

YOUNG MAN: *(Scared)* How . . . how did I lie?

TALL MAN: You pretended innocence—that is the only way you could speak about the bomb; say the things you said about it, by feigning ignorance. You want people to believe you, and who is there does not believe in innocence? I know a person like you, he feigned innocence about the same thing you are portraying innocence about, the bomb. At this moment he's in the loony bin, and do you know why?

YOUNG MAN: *(Timidly)* Why?

TALL MAN: Because it backfired on him, that's why. It got so that he actually believed all that balderdash he was putting down. So involved did he become with the bomb, to such a peak of madness, that he was convinced that he was the bomb. Yes! With these very

ears did I hear him confide to me: "I tell you it is up to me whether the bomb falls or not! If the bad in me wins out the bomb will fall! If the good in me wins out the bomb will not fall—" Dangerous business, this making the bomb one's way of life, dangerous!

YOUNG MAN: *(At first awkwardly, then gaining courage)* I'm no bomb. I don't want to be the bomb. You have me all wrong, you—Sir, you presume to know me not knowing me. I don't respect presumption, even when it is true.

TALL MAN: Do you deny you were pretending innocence?

YOUNG MAN: *(Standing up straight, fearlessly)* When I am innocent I do not know I am being innocent—but as soon as I do become aware of it, I get a terribly empty feeling all over, I get scared, and want to run home and never leave the house again. And besides, why shouldn't I talk to people about bombs and things, it's what's happening to us this day and age, isn't it? Look, there go the Ban The Bomb, No Shelter, marchers—are they pretending? No. So it's good to talk about it, and say and do what you feel is right about it. Good, all of it good. Everything is good, and I don't care if you think I'm lying. All I know is I had little stars and angels in my hair a while ago, and now I don't.

TALL MAN: *(Shaking his head)* Then you are an absurd innocent, my friend; because everything is not good, all is not good; but I don't doubt it makes you feel good to say it.

YOUNG MAN: *(Getting scared again)* You're right, you're right, all is not good—I only say it to make myself happy, I guess.

TALL MAN: Take my advice, forget about the bomb, I can see it in your face, the same thing I saw in that poor chap's face; and at this moment he's sitting in some padded cell hoping not to explode. Human beings are unpredictable; anything can happen.

YOUNG MAN: *(Noticeably worried)* Yes, that's what I'm always saying, anything can happen, and often does.

TALL MAN: Good-by.

YOUNG MAN: *(Terribly brought down)* Yes, good-by.

He sags against the street light determined never to stand on a street corner again, determined never to be unaware of himself, of anything, ever again—

YOUNG MAN: A human bomb—yes, things like that can happen, anything can happen; he said it happened! I better go home. I better get a taxi. Taxi!

A little girl comes up to him.

LITTLE GIRL: Mister, could you please take me across?

Taxi stops. He hesitates.

YOUNG MAN: *(Paying no mind to the street light)* Okay, but let's hurry, I gotta go home.

He takes her hand, and begins to cross street.

The play might end with a car running them both down or it could end with him taking her across safely, it very well could end that way.

DRAWINGS BY THE AUTHOR

Sarpedon

(1954)

Corso's prefatory comments to his reading of Sarpedon *at the Naropa Institute, July 20, 1978**

Anybody know Sarpedon? Oh, okay. Sarpedon was known in America about four years ago [1974] by the calyx krater made by Euphronios 5 B.C. Sarpedon is dead, you see. It's the death of Sarpedon. Between him is Hypnos and Thanatos. Death and Sleep. In 1954 I wrote it—24 years ago—that's when I first hit Harvard. Mr. Finley, a great Greek scholar, was running Eliot House and I was told by one of his TAs, if I could write a Greek play I could stay at Eliot House. I did it overnight. Now the way you do it, you take the Homeric hit like Aeschylus, Sophocles, Euripides. They all played on it. So I played on this ballgame.

Sarpedon is the son of Europa and Zeus. Remember the paintings of Titian and Rubens? Over the water the bull is taking the woman? Well, he's the son. Okay. He's on the side of the Trojans. Remember the water.

*Corso, Gregory. "Socratic Poetry Rap 7/20/1978." *JKS Audio Collection.* (Boulder, Colorado: Naropa University Archives, 1978): <http://cdm16621.contentdm.oclc.org/cdm/ref/collection/p16621coll1/id/2203>. Corso refers to the "Sarpedon krater" controversy that resulted in the Metropolitan Museum of Art repatriating Euphronios' famous vase. The krater was actually created c. 515 B.C, and not 5 B.C. as Corso suggested.

Poseidon, the god of the water, is for the Trojans. Zeus, the daddy of the skies. Hades, the third brother, the underworld. Okay, this is how I created it.

Being they're gonna have their war, Hades gets all the dead on the fields of Troy. Now, remember what I told you that's on this big calyx krater that made noise four years ago in New York in the Metropolitan. They ripped it off. They paid two mill for it. Okay.

"Sar-*PEE*-don." Not saltpeter. I could say "*SAR*-pe-don" but my rhyme goes "Sar-*PEE*-don." All right.

****

It is agreed. There will be war.
Zeus the Greeks.
Poseidon the Trojans.
And Hades the Dead.

The entrance of the Underworld. In the dim misty light of dawn, the Roll Caller, standing beside Charon, is calling the names of the new dead. Hades, checking the dead that file past him, stands to the left of Charon.

ROLL CALLER: Orsilochos, Ormenos, Daitor, Chromios.
Melanippos, Lycophontes, Archeptolemos.

CHARON: That does it.

ROLL CALLER: I counted 70.

CHARON: That's correct. Let's be off.

HADES: Wait! 71.
My list has it 71.

CHARON: You want us to make a recount?

HADES: I know who's missing.
Sarpedon. Where is he? He's due.

CHARON: True.

HADES: Well . . . where is he?

CHARON: Don't ask me.

HADES: What do you mean, "don't ask me"?
Who am I supposed to ask?

CHARON: I don't like the tone of your voice.

HADES: Fool! You expect me to rejoice?
Sarpedon is mine now that's he's dead.

CHARON: I bring you all the dead I get
—in and out of season.
Mine's a lousy job. I get all wet.
Yet you curse me for not bringing Sarpedon.
Look at me all smelly and drippy with rot;
that's the thanks I get joining your miserable lot.
You think because you gave me a silver oar
for Zeusmas I am indebted to you,
well you're mistaken;
if you can chew the ham you can fry the bacon.

HADES: Keep Menelaus's tags out of this.

CHARON: I warn you Hades if you keep tormenting me
treating me like a delivery boy
I'll cease to bring the dead to be
from the gory fields of Troy.

HADES: Charon, all I want is my due.
Sarpedon is mine, and that's true.

CHARON: True or no, you insulted me.
I never use tags used by others.
You have no right to say I do.
Do you doubt I created:
Men may be gods but they'll never be mothers?

HADES: Every day you bring me cowards and spies
who have fallen on the fields of Troy,
but now that a son of Zeus by Patroclus dies
—I thought surely he'd be on today's envoy.

CHARON: Whoever's on the shore
I pick up. That's my job, no more.
Who they be; swineherds or sons of Zeus, I care not.
Dead they're all the same or have you forgot?

HADES: Sarpedon is special.
He's unlike the common mortal.
His mother was Europa
and his father, a bull.

CHARON: I know the story.

HADES: Then I want Sarpedon!

CHARON: There were 70 on shore.
Only 70—no more.
Ah yes, Hephaestus was there.
He made a cup for you—here.

HADES: A cup? For me? What did he say?

CHARON: Happy birthday.

HADES: It is my birthday! Good old Hephaestus.

ROLL CALLER: Hadn't we better get a move on?

CHARON: Yes.

HADES: No! No one leaves! Not until
I find out what became of Sarpedon.
You're up to something Charon.
I warn you, be careful
or you'll be sorry.

CHARON: How's this. Sorry?
Who's going to make me sorry?

HADES: No one. All I want . . .

CHARON: How are you going to make me sorry?

HADES: If I don't get Sarpedon
you'll soon see how.

CHARON: Well, just for that Sarpedon you'll never see.
I'll let him stand on the shore
no matter how much you or he implore.
He'll stay there! In the black mist he'll toss!
And I dare him defy me and swim across!
I'll teach you to threaten me
you gloomy husband to Persephone.

HADES: I didn't mean to threaten you.
O I am the saddest of the gods!
Poseidon has his earthquakes
and Zeus his lightning rods
and I—I have you.
And what do you do?
Treat me as you would the dead
and call me gloomy to the wife I wed.

CHARON: All right, all right, stop cryin.
I can't bear to hear those tears of iron.

Exit Charon and Roll Caller

HADES: Fish head! Wait, someday I'll show him
damn! If only the dead were able to swim!

Enter Persephone

PERSEPHONE: What are you mumbling about?

HADES: Shhh must you shout?
What will the guards think?
O if only his boat would sink!

PERSEPHONE: Charon? Ha! What would you do without Charon?
You pray he drowns? Ha! Go, pray on.
Surely the dead will swim across that ink.
And I don't give a fig for what the guards think.
I'm mistress here, aye, Queen! and I do as I please.

HADES: All right. Enough! Geez—
must everybody pounce on me like this?
First it's Sarpedon I miss
then Charon with his disrespect
and now you, what next to expect?
And why haven't you given the newly dead their linen?
Look at them hanging around waiting to be fed.
Go, console them, entertain them;
play them my latest requiem.

PERSEPHONE: Who are you married to anyway

me or the dead?
You hardly notice me anymore;
not even in bed.

HADES: A god finds joy in many things
the joys of the bed are all right
but a god knows greater things
such as counting bones in the night.

PERSEPHONE: Great joy.

HADES: Besides, there's much to be done;
as of now there's Sarpedon.

PERSEPHONE: What a lovely cup!
Is it for me? From my mother?

HADES: Hands off! Hephaestus gave it to me
for my birthday; it's mine.
But what a birthday! I'm so unhappy!
I wanted him so terribly much.
Among mortal men he's Zeus' proudest son.
I'm sick of champion bowmen
spies cowards and such.
That's all I've been getting!
My kingdom's become a rat nest!
Well I'll get him I swear I'll not rest!

PERSEPHONE: You didn't even notice my new hair-do.

HADES: Why should I? Besides, I don't care to.
Did you remember my birthday?

PERSEPHONE: You're a cold god, Hades.

Enter Ormenos

ORMENOS: Hey, where are all the ladies?

HADES: Guards! Get this ass out of here!

PERSEPHONE: Look, there's Charon!

HADES: O Charon you brought Sarpedon!

CHARON: No—Hector.

PERSEPHONE: O he's much better than Sarpedon!

CHARON: The best!

HECTOR: Good but not good enough, that's me.
Prince of Troy! Joy to Andromache!
Much feared was I, this the Argives know.
See my sword? See the red blood glow!
Many battles this sword for me has won. . . .

HADES: Take him back!

CHARON: *What?*

HADES: I want Sarpedon!

CHARON: Can't be done.

HECTOR: Ah Persephone!
You are as I imagined you to be,
are you not Aphrodite?

PERSEPHONE: O sweetest of husbands
do let Hector stay!

HADES: No! I don't trust that Priam family.
Wife-stealers, that's what they are, all of them!

PERSEPHONE: O don't be silly
who would want to steal me?

CHARON: It's getting so I don't like coming here anymore.
I thought I was doing you a favor by bringing Hector.
I've a good mind to go and complain to Zeus!
Damnit, I will!

Exit Charon

HADES: What do I care of Zeus?
I own my own religion!
Go ahead, go tell him,
you stool-pigeon!

The following day Hermes is sent to Hades by Zeus.

HERMES: Okay, what's up? Zeus sent me.
He doesn't like to see Charon upset.
What did you do to him? No mind.
Zeus wants to know what's troubling you.
Say what you have to say, and let things be done.

HADES: Tell him I didn't get Sarpedon.
Tell him it was agreed that my share of the war
was to have all the dead. And Sarpedon is dead!
Tell him if I don't get Sarpedon I'll close my doors!
Tell him the dead will pile up!
Tell him—*what*? What have you there?

HERMES: Where?

HADES: There! Behind your back.
Ah! I caught you!
O Zeus is this how you go about finding what's up?
This pest tried to steal Hephaestus' cup!

Thief! Thief! Give it back!

HERMES: Easy, man.
I didn't steal it
I only wanted to feel it.
Everybody's always accusing me.
I'm your guest;
you're supposed to be amusing me.

HADES: Don't give me that!
I know your sob stories.
You're a thief through and through.
As soon as you were born
you stole Hyperion's cows;
now tell me that's not true.

HERMES: Please, don't bug me about my youth.

HADES: It's the truth, isn't it? The truth!

HERMES: Man, you're nowhere.
No wonder poor Charon was in such despair.

Exit Hermes

HADES: Guard!

GUARD: Good thing you called. The dead,
there's unrest; they want to be fed.

HADES: My wife does nothing; work is piling up.
The dead are hungry and the tables bare.
Here hide this cup
else it end in the sink
with the rest of the silverware.

GUARD: Should I go get your wife?

HADES: Bah! Let her be.
I've got to do something.
Can't let them get away with this.
Sarpedon! Sarpedon! Sarpedon!

GUARD: True. Sarpedon is a painful worry.
And there are things to think about
and things to forget.
But shouldn't something be done?
The dead are very hungry; especially Dolon.
He screams the loudest. I fear revolt.

HADES: What? Dolon! That disgusting spy! Revolt!
Fetch him at once!
I'll show him who's who down here.

Exit Guard

Enter Guard with Dolon

DOLON: Ah Hades most illustrious god
I come on behalf of my fellow dead;
as their spokesman, we demand . . .

HADES: Shut up! How dare you?
You come because I have ordered it so!
Spy! Miscreant!
Hector is here;
he has not forgotten how you bungled your mission.
Achilles' horses, indeed!
Oxen is too good for you, incompetent ass!

DOLON: Hector forgives,
and that's more one could say for you.

HADES: O that Odysseus and Diomedes had left
your carcass to rot in the sun!

DOLON: Rumor has it you'll not get Sarpedon.
Rumor has it he's in Elysium.

VOICES OF THE DEAD: Food! Clean cerements! New requiems! Rusty nails!

HADES: Persephone! Persephone!

GUARD: Don't expect her to come.
She and Hector are a twosome.
Together they pluck dead flowers
and watch the little bats make love,
and sometimes they watch for hours
like two fingers in a one-finger glove.

HADES: I knew it! Asphodels! I knew he'd steal her!
O Zeus, you cow-eater! I'll make you pay!
It's all your fault! I won't be treated this way!
Isn't your wife enough? Must you have mine too?
I know you've taken Hector's form! Bastard!
Rape artist! You can't fool me!
How would you like it if somebody raped your wife?
It could happen; it could just happen!
And I'm the one to do it too!

DOLON: This bickering over ladies
ain't gonna feed the dead, Hades.

HADES: Away! Leave me alone.
I am the saddest of gods.
No one loves me.
No one sacrifices anything to me.
All they do is cheat! Hermes steals my cup;
Charon doesn't bring me Sarpedon,
and that cow-eater rapes my wife!

GUARD: Why don't you go up
and have it out with him?

HADES: I'll just do that!
Get me a bat.

GUARD: The bats are making love.

HADES: Hang it! I'll go without one.

Olympus. Hades is standing before Zeus who is in a great hurry.

HADES: Here you are, don't deny what you've done!
You raped my wife and stole Sarpedon!

ZEUS: Can't talk now, got to run.
20 cows in Ethiopia;
I'm starved. Come again.
Sarpedon? See Europa.
Sorry, can't introduce her.

Exit Zeus

HADES: How he treats me! Am I not as powerful as he?
Ah, there's his wife. I'll show him!
Just a little closer and then I'll pounce on her!

He pounces on who he thinks to be Hera but who is actually Aphrodite.

APHRODITE: Hel———p!

Enter Hephaestus

HEPHAESTUS: O Hades is this the thanks I get?
This is the worst seduction of my wife yet!
And after I spent two months on that cup for you.

HADES: O dear
It was an error
I had no idea
I thought it was Hera.

APHRODITE: I'm not to blame this time, Hephaestus.
Remember when Ares—and what you did to us?

HEPHAESTUS: I want my cup back!

HADES: But . . . but . . .

HEPHAESTUS: And my fire! You'll get no more heat from me!

Back in his dark kingdom Hades sits dejected on his throne.

VOICES OF THE DEAD: Heat! Food! Warmer cerements!

DOLON: Hades, the dead need heat!

HADES: What about me?
Look at my feet, how blue!
I've never been so cold!

What am I to do?

DOLON: If there's no fire
couldn't we have food at least?
Nothing much, just some rusty wire
even oily rags will do.
We don't expect a feast;
and I'm sorry your feet are blue.

GUARD: Hades, the Styx has turned to ice!

DOLON: Even bent nails will suffice.

GUARD: Charon says he's not going to skate across.

DOLON: It isn't as if we were asking for steak.

Enter Persephone

PERSEPHONE: What is this I hear—Aphrodite?
Well! from now on
don't expect me to keep things tidy.

DOLON: Madam, we are cold.

PERSEPHONE: Indeed the weather is not pleasing.
I guess something should be done.
My dead flowers are freezing
—who's this, Sarpedon?

DOLON: I am Dolon, spokesman for the dead.
We need food and heat and cerements.

Enter Hermes

HERMES: I've come for Hephaestus's cup.

I didn't think you had it in you. How was it?

HADES: How was what?

HERMES: Aw, come off it man, you know what I mean.
Aphrodite. I take my petasos* off to you,
she's the immortal end.

HADES: It was a mistake, a terrible mistake!

HERMES: Sure, man, sure.

HADES: Leave me alone you degenerate!

DOLON: Food! Heat!

HADES: A mistake! A mistake!

PERSEPHONE: Look at him brag!

VOICES OF THE DEAD: Give us back life!

END

*Editor's note: A *petasos* was a style of hat with a low crown and broad brim worn by ancient Greek travelers and hunters. The god Hermes was often represented in art wearing a winged petasos.

In This Hung-Up Age

A One-Act Farce Written in 1954

Synopsis:

The year is 1954 and a Greyhound bus leaves from New York on its way to San Francisco. None of the passengers know each other, and are going to San Francisco for different reasons, except the POETMAN who is following BEAUTY. Three days out of New York and the bus breaks down.

List of Characters

HIPSTER: *A New York City lower East Side delinquent, tough and endowed with slang and jazz talk, twenty years old; wears loud clothes*

TOURIST: *A red-necked Midwest square, middle-aged*

MRS. KINDHEAD: *Progressive Liberal Housewife do-gooder type, middle-aged or a little over*

POETMAN: *Little-magazine type with social complaints, drinks, bemoans the plight of poesy, and wears sloppy but clean clothes, twenty years old*

APACHE: *American Indian, philosophical jazz enthusiast, thirty-five years old*

College Girl: *Radcliffe College, prim, sharp, naive, nineteen years old*

Bus Driver: *Greyhound bus driver, courteous, middle-aged*

Beauty: *Dressed in white gown, she never says anything, takes sleeping pills, occasionally blows on saxophone*

****

Bus Driver: Be patient, folks . . . nothing too serious. We're not out of gas. Whatever it is I'll have it fixed in a jiffy. *(He fidgets with the dashboard.)*

Hipster: What a drag.

Tourist: What a God-forsaken place to be stuck in!

Mrs. Kindhead: It seems like a desert.

Bus Driver: No need to fear; we're on the main highway. . . .

Tourist: A pretty sick highway if you ask me. Where are all the cars?

Bus Driver: They're around. Not much as they used to be but they're still around. See? There goes one now.

Tourist: Well, why didn't you go out and stop it!

Bus Driver: Now just relax; it's probably the motor; I'll have it fixed in a jiffy.
(He goes out to check motor.)

Tourist: Probably! It's "probably the motor" he says!

Hipster: *(Snarling at the Tourist to whom he's taken an immediate dislike)* He said relax, didn't he?

The Tourist replies with a do-I-know-you look. Meanwhile the Poetman takes out a pint of whisky and gulps it down. Beauty blows a few notes on her saxophone. She sits at the back of the bus.

APACHE: In this hung-up age not much great Poetman can do. Beauty gone mad. All time from New York she blow saxophone not so good; me know good saxophone or not. *(The Poetman sails over to Beauty and sits cross-legged beneath her.)* Poor Poetman, what he understand? She speak like Greek; takes sleeping pills; I hope Beauty go to California for health.

HIPSTER: Looks like Poetman's got eyes for her.

APACHE: Great Poetman he all time follow her. She not see his eyes. Heap gloom. Heap gloom.

TOURIST: *(Laughing at something in his* Saturday Evening Post*)* Ha ha ha ha! Boy, that Winchell's sure got them commies pegged right! Nothing but a bunch of Chinese opium eaters he calls them! OOOooha!

HIPSTER: Whata you so anti-semitic against the Chinese for, man?

TOURIST: Do I know you?

HIPSTER: *(Tapping the Apache on the shoulder)* Seems like we got a cornball on the bus, chief.

POETMAN: *(Feeling the edge of Beauty's gown)* Why do you keep on taking those sleeping pills for? You're hardly ever awake; is it that bad?

APACHE: Poor Poetman.

HIPSTER: Well, like listen, man, what do you expect? In this hung-up age what's the sense of the guy writing all that boid an tree stuff when there ain't nobody to listen? In fact, even Beauty wants to fall asleep on him!

APACHE: Great Poetman no care if no one listen.

HIPSTER: Like face it, man, a poet's gotta be heard. Without a audience the cat's like a chicken without a head—beat—nowhere, dead, man, dead.

TOURIST: Hogwash! Haven't you two vagabonds watched the great plains and cities we've passed these last two days? There's your poetry! What's the Poetman think: he's the only one with the right to talk? Hogwash, I say. Besides, I for one think poets a menace. A lot of them write Communistic propaganda our school kids read about these days. Twisting their minds with all sorts of Chinese symbols. Well, I'm glad we Americans don't listen!

MRS. KINDHEAD: I listen. My name is Mrs. Kindhead, and I'm for progress, any kind. Now, if Mr. Poetman has anything to say, I'd gladly listen. What have you to say, Mr. Poetman?

POETMAN: There isn't any politics in a poet's life, and Winchell be damned. *(He drinks.)* And God, Liberace, and oilmen, be damned! It's them twisting the minds of kids, and I don't write Chinese symbols, that's what I've got to say.

HIPSTER: *(To Tourist, with a very offended expression on his face)* Hey, what do you mean by calling me a vagabond before? It just hit me that you were trying to say I was a bum or something!

The Tourist ignores him; without the Tourist seeing him the Hipster sticks his tongue out at him.

MRS. KINDHEAD: *(To Poetman)* Is that all you've got to say?

POETMAN: Okay *(Takes more to drink)* I'll say more. In this hung-up age Beauty hasn't been altogether forgotten. But with all these movie, radio, and television creeps around, one's almost inclined to forget her. And the funny thing is that Beauty herself would urge us to forget. Can you blame her for being beat? Look at America today, look at what's happening!

TOURIST: Hogwash! That drunk doesn't make any sense at all—and if he doesn't like it here why doesn't he go to Russia. Go to Russia if you don't like it.

HIPSTER: *(To Tourist)* Listen, mister, who's askin' you to listen for?

POETMAN: *(Holding his bottle high up)* To Louella Parsons, the witch!

COLLEGE GIRL: I see no reason why a poet should concern himself with such inane things—

POETMAN: Inane, is it? Listen, girl, Louella is the mammoth madam of our emotions. She's worse than a Nero, and do you want to know why? I'll tell you why. She's a dictator of the mind, that's why. She whores you off to a phony dream world that oozes over with a gush and sentiment, a peaches and cream world that doesn't even have a john in it—when she shows you the moon she shows you an Alice Faye moon, not the moon. Well, she can't fool me, they aren't going to get my emotions they're not. No wonder poets sing of rotten things today. What good the singer who sings who does not sing *his* song?

COLLEGE GIRL: You're bitter over nothing. I don't understand you poets. Are you men? You always want to be understood, as if you were something other than people. Are you men? What are you then? Why don't you learn a trade, to call a spade a spade? In any age a man has got to work to live; he has no time for explanations; and, if I can be somewhat poetical myself, I would say lamentations rather than explanations. Yes, why don't you learn a trade, learn to call a spade a spade—

HIPSTER: That chick is looking for some cat to work for her. As for me, I always call a spade a spade—if he is a spade.

POETMAN: That's just what I was trying to get at! Today poets are frightened, afraid to call a spade a spade. It's what I've been trying to say all along: What good the singer who does not sing his song? *(Beauty blows on her sax.)*

TOURIST: *(Irritated by it)* Good God, what in vinegar is that! *(Beauty blows louder and screechier.)* Cut that hogwash out!

APACHE: Beauty gone mad. Poetman gone mad. He try to

fight nature; he lose. Nature all right without Poetman; Poetman no all right without nature. And him who all time say hogwash, him without hope.

TOURIST: What in hell is that aborigine talking about? What does he know of this age?

MRS. KINDHEAD: I should think quite a fair amount, sir.

TOURIST: And who in hell are you?

MRS. KINDHEAD: My name is Mrs. Kindhead, and I'm all for progress, any kind. What you don't seem to realize is that men like you prevent progress; men like you just ain't with it.

HIPSTER: *(Slapping Kindhead on back)* Crazy, lady, crazy.

APACHE: Mrs. Kindhead gone mad now. She first liberal, now she hipster. No good, no good this hung-up age.

COLLEGE GIRL: *(To Poetman)* There's something I would like to get straight. When you people talk about hung-up age, hung-up for whom? The poet, or for everyone?

TOURIST: What in hell is that bus driver up to! He said a jiffy, didn't he? A jiffy!

POETMAN: For everyone. Doesn't it show? Don't you realize what's been happening in the last ten years? Look at the babe born today in this age—as soon as he is able to walk his Liberace loving parents wouldn't think of giving him Latin and Greek, no because that doesn't make money, so they send him off to school for a terrible knowledge. If once in school he dreams, if once he tires of trivial things, "lazy lazy!" the teacher screams, while all the while in his little heart an ocean sings—

TOURIST: How corny can you get!

HIPSTER: Shud up, y'creep.

TOURIST: Watch your step, sonny, that's all I've got to say, watch your step.

HIPSTER: Aw, go eat a dead frog.

COLLEGE GIRL: Now really, Poetman, you haven't made it at all clear. If this age is hung-up, it certainly is not the fault of a teacher calling a potential poet lazy.

POETMAN: It's not all of it, but it's got a lot to do with it—they're educating kids today to do anything but dream.

COLLEGE GIRL: In other words you attribute this age a mystery, something like, er, like the trinity of God, right?

POETMAN: What?

APACHE: Seems College Girl go mad too.

HIPSTER: *(To Apache, pointing at Beauty)* Hey, Tonto, wot's up wid dat chick in the corner do you think she's really flipped? Like one thing's certin, she can't blow dat horn she's got. But just dig her legs, willya!

APACHE: She Beauty, Poetman chase her all his life; she no stop. She on her way to California.

HIPSTER: To Hollywood?

APACHE: Nope. To Frisco. In Frisco she hope to lose Poetman by joining jazz band.

HIPSTER: How? She can't play a crumby note!

APACHE: Don't worry. Beauty learn fast. Beauty like buffalo meat, easy to eat.

HIPSTER: Huh?

MRS. KINDHEAD: *(Quite attracted to the Apache)* Sir, you're something of a philosopher; I'm amazed by your metaphor.

APACHE: Me just Apache.

MRS. KINDHEAD: How shameful it is that we took this country away from you. If anyone's a true American, it is you, sir.

TOURIST: Ha! That's a laugh!

MRS. KINDHEAD: It's true!

TOURIST: Hogwash! We won it fair and square.

HIPSTER: Yeah, square's just the woid, pops.

APACHE: Me just Apache.

POETMAN: *(Drunkenly, to anyone)* The real truth of the matter is, if you want to know why this age is hung-up, is because people are too damn cheap to buy a poetry magazine—

HIPSTER: Hey, chief, tell me, did the Apaches really fight like dey show in the movies?

APACHE: Me pacifist.

MRS. KINDHEAD: Amazing! And we dare say you're not civilized!

TOURIST: *(Muttering)* Commies, I knew it! the whole lot of them, commies! *(Beauty begins to blow sax again.)* Hey, miss, why don't you play that thing outside?

And what in hell is that bus driver doing out there! Never, never again will I take another damn bus! Idiots! All of them, nuts!

HIPSTER: Boy, mister, y'lucky y'ain't walkin down my neighborhood. It's cats like you make juvenile delinquents outa innocent people—

TOURIST: *(Red in the face)* Keep it up, sonny, just keep it up.

HIPSTER: Y'scare me.

MRS. KINDHEAD: Do you live on a reservation?

APACHE: Me live in furnished room; pay five dollar a week.

MRS. KINDHEAD: Oh.

Long silence

POETMAN: Sure. A lot of people hang up Picasso prints and all that just to show how modern and intellectual they are, but just once, just once would I like to see them buy a poetry magazine. They're phonies, cheats, penny pinchers! That's why this age is hung-up, it's because of them!

COLLEGE GIRL: How way off you are.

POETMAN: Why years ago a poet used to be treated like a king! If he was hungry all doors were opened for him! If he wanted a woman, fifty women came. If one day he dared stain his hands with work, the whole world wept in shame!

COLLEGE GIRL: *(To Hipster)* You sound New York.

HIPSTER: Right on the button, baby. Where you from?

COLLEGE GIRL: From Cambridge, Mass.

HIPSTER: What's happening there?

COLLEGE GIRL: Did you ever hear of Harvard?

HIPSTER: You mean the school? I thought it wuz only for cats.

COLLEGE GIRL: Cats?

HIPSTER: *(Annoyed)* Men, boys, guys. God, wotta square.

COLLEGE GIRL: I'm sorry if you seem slightly obtuse to me.

HIPSTER: *(Pushing back his duck-assed hair)* I seen worser lookin' cats.

COLLEGE GIRL: I did not mean your appearance. No. I don't go to Harvard. I go to Radcliffe. I guess you've never heard of Radcliffe?

HIPSTER: I heard of some things.

COLLEGE GIRL: Yes. Well, Radcliffe is a girls' college; it's juxtaposed with Harvard.

HIPSTER: You don't say? Say, that's a crazy-looking blouse you got on, baby. What's it, silk? *(He feels her blouse, she pushes his hand away.)*

COLLEGE GIRL: It's linen.

HIPSTER: You mean what they make sheets out of? Me, I got silk. Imported. Here look. *(He bends his neck in an effort to show her the collar label.)*

COLLEGE GIRL: *(Not looking)* I believe you.

HIPSTER: Me, I sort of dig crazy clothes. What's your name?

COLLEGE GIRL: Guess.

HIPSTER: *(Perplexed, and bugged)* Guess? An you say you go to college? If that ain't the stupidest—guess? How the heck can I guess somebody's name when I don't know that somebody? Baby, you're too much. *(He turns away from her, mockingly.)* Bon swah!

TOURIST: *(Yelling out of window)* Hey driver, what in the name of Jesus are you doing out there! It's been an hour already! Is that your idea of a jiffy?

BUS DRIVER: *(Outside)* Pretty soon, folks, pretty soon.

POETMAN: They walk around in their gray flannel suits and think that makes them lovers of poetry. They're like turtles, cowards! hiding in a shell.

TOURIST: Oh, hell!

APACHE: Soon everybody go mad. Bus no more; buffalo no more—me go mad too, I guess.

MRS. KINDHEAD: Oh, no. It's not all that bad. Courage, sir, courage! After all, we're all in the same boat, bus, so to speak, ha-ha.

TOURIST: Corny hag.

MRS. KINDHEAD: I heard you, sir, and I resent what I heard.

APACHE: This is not just atomic age, this also hung-up age. No hope. Everything like buffalo milk, good, then turn bad.

MRS. KINDHEAD: Such insight!

TOURIST: Did I get on the wrong bus? Did I make a mistake and get on a loony bus instead? *(He puts his head out the window again.)* Hurry up, you clumsy ass!

BUS DRIVER: *(Outside)* Easy, mister. The bus driving school of etiquette does not say anything about taking anyone's guff. Just hold your horses.

HIPSTER: Ha, ha. I guess he put you down, but good.

TOURIST: I'm almost inclined to get out and walk!

HIPSTER: Why don'tcha, why don'tcha.

POETMAN: My poems will renew hope, and more! Only a poet can renew hope! It is the rose that seeks in the rose a flaw.

APACHE: Poetman got heap talent. Him now rose. Me, I no talent. Me just Apache.

COLLEGE GIRL: *(To Tourist)* Do you live in California?

TOURIST: *(Bluntly)* No!

HIPSTER: How can you have eyes to talk to a creep like dat, baby? He probably even hates his mudder.

At this point the Tourist, red as a beet, hits the Hipster on the head with his rolled-up Saturday Evening Post. *Small entanglement; both fall; women scream; driver rushes in; he and Apache separate the two contestants.*

BUS DRIVER: The bus driving school has given me the right to put off anyone caught fighting or disturbing the peace on this bus. Now let's not have it happen again. Good God, can't you people be patient like people? I'm almost done now, so be patient! *(He goes out.)*

TOURIST: *(Crying)* You hoodlum! I happen to love my mother more than anything else in the world. If more people thought of their mothers the way I do there'd be less talk of hogwash and hung-up ages!

HIPSTER: I don't talk t'cornballs.

POETMAN: Back to the womb! I advocate back to the womb!
It's the only panacea for this hung-up age.
We must all be born again.
We must all come out great lovers of poetry.
(Falls in drunken stupor.)

APACHE: Him now go back to womb. Him can. Him got womb. So hogwash man. Me got no mother. Me can't come out great liker of poetry.

MRS. KINDHEAD: *(Putting her arm around Apache)* Oh you poor thing. No mother! How sad life must be for you. I wish in some way, in some form or miracle that I could, by the will of God, be your mother.

APACHE: Me not know what to say about that.

HIPSTER: I feel a romance comin on.

Beauty blows her sax again.

TOURIST: Oh God! Oh God! Oh God!

COLLEGE GIRL: *(To Tourist)* If you don't live in California, where do you live?

TOURIST: *(Completely despaired)* I don't know, I don't know any more!

APACHE: This age impossible without saxophone. Without saxophone is like buffalo without tail.

HIPSTER: What's the buffalo always got to do with it?

APACHE: Buffalo to me what camel to Arab.

TOURIST: It's night, it's night out there!

Short silence

HIPSTER: Hey, Mrs. Kindhead, what are you gonna do in California, if we ever get there?

MRS. KINDHEAD: Look for progress, any kind.

TOURIST: *(Infuriated)* Lady, do you know what progress stands for, do you? It stands for communism, that's what! Don't you know we're at war with communism, don't you!

She raises her head, defiantly ignoring him.

APACHE: Not much progress it seem. Me once have vision, me see buffalo walk backward.

A tremendous noise outside

BUS DRIVER: *(Running into bus, frantically closing door)* A raging bison!

HIPSTER: A what?

BUS DRIVER: A berserk buffalo! It came charging after me!

COLLEGE GIRL: Is the bus fixed?

BUS DRIVER: Almost. It was almost fixed.

HIPSTER: *(Looking out of window)* It's bangin' its horns against the motor!

BUS DRIVER: My bus!

TOURIST: Go out and kill the Goddam thing!

HIPSTER: Boy, look at it foam from the mouth!

BUS DRIVER: Let's wave to the cars for help!

TOURIST: What cars! There haven't been any cars!

HIPSTER: Hey, chief, you know buffaloes, why don'tcha go out and talk to it or somethin'?

APACHE: No can do. Heap gloom. It all right if everybody go mad, but if buffalo go mad, heap gloom.

TOURIST: Then kill it! Just don't stand there!

APACHE: Me no kill, me pacifist.

TOURIST: What did I do to deserve this? What???

HIPSTER: Let's send Beauty out; maybe she can do somethin'—y'know, Beauty and the Beast?

BUS DRIVER: No, she'd get torn to shreds, it's my duty to protect the passengers.

TOURIST: Then protect us, damnit!

APACHE: This hung-up age hung-up no more. Buffalo soon

bring everything down. We all go to happy hunting grounds.

COLLEGE GIRL: This is absurd. One shabby buffalo can't do all that harm.

APACHE: Soon many more come—there! Look!

Great stampede! Herds and herds of buffalo charge the bus.

TOURIST: They look insane!

HIPSTER: I thought them things was extinct?

COLLEGE GIRL: They're coming right at the bus! At us!

Everyone screams. Lights go out. The bus is trampled over. Thunderous noise of hoofs and steel and human cries. Slowly the stampede fades—moans and groans.

COLLEGE GIRL: Help—

POETMAN: Apocalypse—

BUS DRIVER: My bus—

APACHE: This good-by—

TOURIST: I'll sue, I'll sue—

MRS. KINDHEAD: My little cats, who'll take care of my little cats—

HIPSTER: Man, what a draggy way to die—

The moon falls full light on Beauty; she and the spot where she sat remain untouched; she blows her saxophone low, soft, and beautifully.

CURTAIN

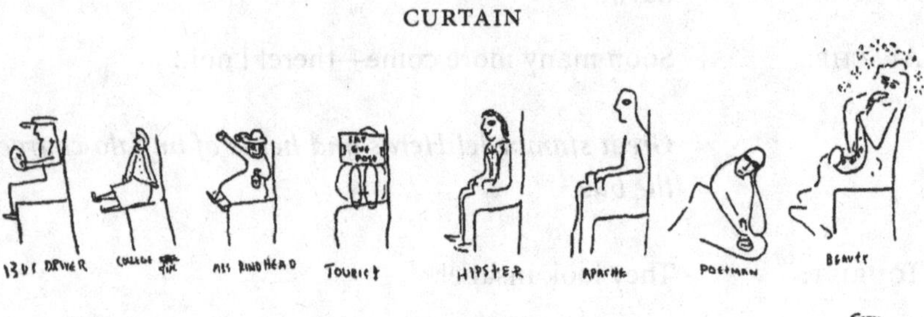

NOTE ON MY PLAY

This play was written in 1954 and was performed April, 1955, at the Harvard Dramatic Workshop by both Harvard and Radcliffe students. I can safely claim that this play, indeed document, pre-dates anything ever written about the Hipster and hip-talk, the Square, and the advent of San Francisco's "poesy rebirth"—all of which came to light in 1956, Mailer 1957, and into a forgotten suitcase for seven years went mine play. So what? So nothing. What is important is this: The late seers of Hip (not Beat) recorded their see *seriously*, whereas I termed this play a farce. I saw the advent and deemed it farce. My Hipster is farcical, my poet is farcical, my square, the entire American social revolution to come, was very real before my eyes seven years ago, but being that I was truly a hipster, the only hip thing to do was to laugh that silly vision straight in the face, and I did. Thus I feel obliged, that I was the first to see and laugh, to be the last to see and laugh: I still hold it a farce. Thank you, Gregorio Nunzio Corso—my full name, which means: The Watchful One, The Announcer, The Way.

—Gregorio Nunzio Corso, 1963

JFK

A Little Verse Play (1960)

Written in Greece 1960 after hearing the acceptance speech of John F Kennedy following the nomination.

Gregory Corso

Round and round the White House walks he
whose heavy thoughts touch no fiscal year
not Russia not Berlin nor things nuclear
Nay but ponders he when and how the moon
And after that   Mars Venus the entire boon

Before his path lands the American eagle
covered in womanish feathers sickly dyed
once might symbol of liberty and pride
atomically mutated into HE-SHE
spermed from the great empire of the 20th century
Produce of the last administration
a pet as it were
and now it's done
Gone with Eisenhower

—Behold! Recognize!
  I was your country your history your sunrise!
  My wings are closing—

Surely the young elect hears the bird
yet seems as though he heard no word
Considers he this emblem he seeks to future
nothing but a beady pesty vulture?

—Regard! I leave for thee an egg   Jack Kennedy
  An egg that might well hatch
  a ratsome wretch!
  Or an egg with life within
  could well prove seraphim
  All depends on how it's sat!—

Up away forever it flies leaving its spawn
the hope of a country hot on the lawn
He picks it up and puts it into a warm pocket
whilst yet pondering the importance of a 6 stage rocket

Ah here comes Senator Oldhat poking about
all crumbled up with the gout

—There are some blind old who give in to the new
  Fools! Don't they know
  where the new begin the old arrive!
  All these *new* around pregnant with cure-alls
  Theirs be a definite miscarriage!   Aye   perdition!—

—Ah Senator! How glad I am to see you
  Boy being President sure makes one wonder a lot
  I've been wondering about the universe Senator
  It's amazing how much we know and yet don't know
  Thus far the apotheosis of all human study
  has served to multiply not lessen the mystery
  All books all charts   all begin with theoretical *Hows*
  and conclude with theological *Whys*—

—How's that? Hows? Whys? Mysteries?—

—It is my contention Senator
that the mystery of life should be given top priority
And I believe the answer rests up there somewhere
Yes before I do anything I must first the moon—

—What about Laos! Berlin! Cuba!—

—Distractions Senator distractions—

—My ears! Something's wrong with my ears!—

—O universe what stripping away? What arriving to?
I am here and I am near!
They who in their mite territories of dissent
stand with pinned-cloth and top hats
are but a photogenic diplomacy
elected to demolish their state or propagate it
They are not anywhere near
The stars Senator the stars are at hand—

—Help! He's gone mad! Citizen Nixon! Citizen Nixon!—

Poor Senator Oldhat fetch Citizen Nixon he will
But hold what with the egg of the eagle?
In a folded hand in his pocket
the young elect gives it all his concern thinking no rocket
He is such could well warm it to birth
are those of different hand shake the earth

While Citizen Nixon in his bathrobe relaxes
eating peanuts and for once nobody's taxes
in rushes Senator Oldhat like a wet cat

—He's selling us to the Reds!
He doesn't want Berlin he wants the moon instead

I tell you he's gone mad!
With these very ears I heard him speak of
mysteries moons heavens! It was fanatical Catholic talk!
It was in poetry! All those Irish are poets!
Dick you've got to do something!   Else all is lost   lost!—

—Senator   retirement has cleared my mind
My position enables me to witness all probabilities
I have made it a necessity   a vow so to speak
that while I endure this mine crisis of temporary retirement
not to adhere to gossip regarding he who retired me—

—Gossip?!   Call you treasonable information   gossip?
Can this be Dick?   You sound like no Dick I know
These are perilous moments!   Look at you
Can that be he lounging in a bathrobe nibbling peanuts!
Rome tells of such noble Romans
dilly-dallying about with parsley in their mouths
Right now that young mad man stands like Nero
with fiddle bow doting on horoscope charts
alchemy books   sitting on an egg!
while America   nay   the *world*! burns red—

—Take hold   Senator   by God are you serious
He speaks of mysteries you say?   Moons?   Eggs?
Catholic mysteries   the Trinity? The Immaculate Conception?
Forgive me   Senator I am grateful to you
Indeed America   yes   as you say   the world   is grateful to you
You have taken me out of my lethargy
If it were not for such news   mad   you say?
Horoscope charts?—

—He's a witch!—

—A witch?—

—I'm a Quaker sir and so are you
We should know a witch when we see one
He'd be a miracle worker He's the meaning of the universe!—

—And he *does* come from Massachusetts
Indeed it seems as though a grand opportunity
is occasioned me
Indeed for I am not content in my bathrobe
moping about the house eating bits of things
hesitant as to whether I feed the dog or not—

—You must bring this to the American people!—

Can this be another crisis for crisis-ridden Nixon?
For surely there's a tricky balance to the proposition
One that could proclaim him the Savior American
Or one that could deny him ever a crisis again
He goes to the fishbowl to think
He winks at the fish the fish doesn't return the wink

—Perhaps this is the true way
I'm no trick judge of men decider of sane insane
but this presumed request for the unknown
does seem an attempt to mitigate in some degree
an immortal pretence seeks he divinity?
Aye best I stand clear
and bide my time endure my defeat
One needs to suffer an entire loss
prior to triumph entire—

—What do you say Richard Nixon
do we impeach the witch?—

—Senator we all play in magic disobedience
accuse some innocent force set hexes upon it

and leave it to awful righteous law
We go straight ahead successantly building pyres
as though it were we who shone on God
and not God on us   considering previous fires
I tell you vengeance will labor us sorely
And that fanciful young man with all his high hopes
can not make the universe a part of America
just because he   quite ephemerally   is good part of it—

—What means all this rhetoric!
I say what are you going to do about this terrible plight?—

—Do about it? Dare I stir my defeat? No
Citizen be citizen
I will hold to my station
I will keep my bathrobe on
I will feed the dog—

The President's office has for decor
plastic rockets looming from the floor
And from the ceiling hang planets
and lots of stars like ariel amulets
He's fixed it so that the radiator
serves the egg as an incubator
The patriotic janitor   just to be sure
took an eagle's bottom's exact temperature
It was a frightfully cold weather
but the young elect braved it with bold sweater
Visitors   kings or boyscouts   on the other hand
not only   because no chairs   had to stand
but also wondered about igloos
and things like Asiatic flus
To make them feel better
he gave them his sweater

Determined was he not to get rooked
into turning up the heat and the egg become cooked

Enters the office Harry Truman
feeling awfully inhuman

—Harry what's wrong?
  You're pale as a ghost—

—I feel like Oedipus!—

—Don't step on the rockets—

—I hate rockets!—

—Would you like my sweater?—

—It's me causing all the ill in the world!
  I shouldn't of done what I did
  At the time it seemed right
  But now now it's all wrong
  The pilots have gone batty
  Was I gave the command
  Was I told em to drop it
  I'm the only man ever to drop it
  Damn be rockets!—

—Hey don't kick them like that
  They're peaceful rockets
  They're for the moon for Mars Venus and beyond—

—I felt right in giving the order
  And I am not one to deny what I felt was right to do
  But that I did it but that I did it
  Oedipus I am!
  Oh that I'd the strength to yank out my eyes!
  But I can break my glasses by God! There!—

—Now why did you go and do a thing like that for?
They're broken—

—Good! I'm glad!   I hope I bump into everything!—

—Life is cruel   Harry   and Time   even crueler
When you did what you did   at the time it seemed right
like you say   and at the time it was Life was cruel not you
But Time uncruels Life   because Life has got to endure
If it remained cruel   then the human race wouldn't be here
So Life   out of necessity   is forgiven
Poor Harry   poor human being   it is not necessary to forgive you
Life suffers not its cruelty
the fortune of so big a thing as is called Life
Poor simple us   we've only ourselves
We stand alone   no thing can help us
Life goes on its merry way   and it'll go on being cruel
And when it stops being cruel   Time takes over
and blames   you
It's Time has hold of life
Setting this up   off-setting that
like some comic-book sinister manipulator
Put destruction into the hands of an uncertainty
and you have it
Life wields Time   Time is Death
Life and Time   awful combo   awful!
Life is   Time does   and after the holocaust
The finger of blame points at you   at man
It can be no other way
Man can't very well blame Time
it's all he's *got*!—

—How wonderful you are
How wonderful is human understanding

I'm sorry about the rockets I'll pick them up—

—These rockets Harry
these rockets are man's only hope
I speak true
With them man can cut Time down to size
Once we rid the world of Time
which again is Death
Once we exchange it for Space
I would say Goodbye cruelty
And isn't that what man has always wanted?
In Space Life is free unbound!
Nobody nothing that is Life dies in Space
We all wait the day
when Life is no longer cruel
I say that day is near
And I am doing my utmost to have us arrive—

—Why's it so cold in here?—

—Would you like my sweater?—

—Is the radiator on?—

—It is—

—Maybe you should turn it up a bit—

—Take my sweater—

—Hey is that your lunch on the radiator?
Boy all that troubling conscience
I can't remember when I last ate—

—I'll order something for you—

—No please don't bother I'll eat at home

but an egg would sure do the trick for the moment
Do you mind?—

—No no no no! Put that egg down!—

—Now what did I do wrong?—

—Eat such an egg?
Why it would mean to eat
all the hope of future eat!
All the cows all the steel all the wheat
all the   it would mean to eat America itself!—

—You're yelling at me   just like everybody else!
All those pretty words of yours
You would deny me an egg even!
How then can God forgive me
when man himself refuses to—

—Harry Truman   this is no ordinary egg
It's not an egg   it's something else
it's—

—Oh it's not an egg
That's why! I see now
Ha ha I mean I *don't* see
I guess I shouldn't of broke my glasses
It looked like an egg—

Ho! and Time alarmed in panic!
For no one who ever fought it won
but now hurt it was by hopes uranic
Indeed the young elect had Time on the run
But the world stopped   chaos pervade
Time demanded Life come to its aid

reminding Life the times it came to the rescue
And Life   all too willing   asked what it could do
Get America Off My Back!
Break Its Leader   Turn That Egg Black!
Ah the egg   *that* Life could do something about
Thus when it opened it was no eagle chick came out
but a full bird   blank black   a shadow
This then is the America the world does know
Everywhere   on buildings on flags on seals
Void in the shape of a bird and a young man's ideals

(Two years later I end play so:
Many a defeat has the President met
To prevent another   he summons his Cabinet

—Gentlemen   the question must be considered
as a part of the worldwide challenge
posed by Communist threats to the peace
. . . it continues to be the policy of the United States
that the Castro regime will not be allowed to export
its aggressive purposes by force or threat of force . . .

END

That Little Black Door on the Left

(circa 1968)

Original Editor's Note: Gregory Corso's That Little Black Door on the Left *will be filmed without dialogue. All of the performances will be pantomime. The only sound track will be musical.*

The condemned man has finished his last meal. The priest and warden are glumly watching him lick his fingers like a gourmet; he has the look of a man who truly enjoyed eating what he had eaten. The warden had told him the bad news, no reprieve; the news did not interrupt his finger-licking. His expression is one of benignity.

He is in his late forties. He stands up. The CAMERA must not show his full body; it must keep on his head, his hands, his legs, but never the body—only when he arrives at the electric chair, then must his body be shown.

The background music is Berlioz' *Requiem*. The lovely, moving, slow, sedate part of that music must play almost throughout; only when he is about to sit in the chair shall the wild great "Tuba Mirum" section blast its trumpets forth.

Two guards come into the scene; one opens the cell door. The doomed man looks at the priest, then the warden, then the guards. He catches all but the priest's eyes—he is rolling off prayers with eyes closed. The warden and guards look back at him with their usual routine look, a look of "We wish this didn't have to be, man, but there's nothing we can do." The warden extends his hand, the doomed shakes it. "Good man, courage," says the warden's face. "Let's get this show on the road," says the doomed's face.

They begin the last mile. It's the same old endless show. The doomed walks upright, unscared but bug-eyed and placid; a little behind him walks the priest, still rolling the prayers; in front of him the warden and the guards. The guards keep their pace, but the warden slows up and turns to face his unfortunate ward with another "Courage, man, courage," looking as though he, and not the condemned, were in need of "Courage, man, courage"—which of course is his well-imbued come-on, making the condemned feel that he's not alone, that someone cares, that it's killing someone else as well.

What can the poor unfortunate do but return a kind of excrement-eating grin? He well knows that the warden doesn't really give a damn. The familiar other doomed ones are also emitting their stock-in-phrase farewells from their miserable cells; he returns them that same kind of grin too, but his doesn't question the sincerity of their farewell. "There but for the grace of God walk the whole miserable bunch." It's themselves they're saying good-bye to; he gives them a wave because he damned well knows they give a damn.

The whole "last mile" scene is to be done entirely from the condemned man's POV—we never see him. It will be shot in the cliché style of the Cagney-Warner Brothers pictures of the 1930s.

They reach the death chamber. From the condemned man's POV we examine the room. It is bare but for one piece of furniture—the "chair" that sits starkly in the center. We now see all who are in attendance. The warden, the priest, the two guards who escorted him, who have been joined by two others, and the executioner.

From the prisoner's POV we near the chair. There are two guards on either side; the executioner stands in front. As he reaches the "chair," the CAMERA now CUTS TO reveal the prisoner's full form—he's the fattest man, or one, of the fattest, in the whole world, like maybe four hundred pounds, and he's not so very tall, so he's wide, vastly wide. Something that has never happened in the entire history of the electric chair now happens: the condemned man's seat is double the size of the seat of the chair. He attempts to sit down but can go no further than his mountainous rear cheeks are able to take him, the chair's arms. A strange, exceedingly unfamiliar dilemma: the guards huffingly and puffingly struggle to squeeze his elephantine buttocks into the chair, trying but not succeeding to stuff those fantastic chops down past the arms of the chair. All the while the great four-hundred-pounder maintains the look of benignity—that is, as long as is humanly possible, what with all those sweating hands trying to stuff him down into the chair like he was the rubber tube of a Mack truck, full blown, surrealistically being stuffed into the tire of a child's tricycle. His face begins to lose its benignity: it is now one of awkward embarrassed hideously comical bulgidity, his eyes popping, his jowls popping, his funnel mouth popping.

And the warden meanwhile is damning the unexpected situation; and the priest truly exclaiming "Oh, God!" and meaning it; and the executioner snarling like a berserk seal who has just lost a much-needed fish to some old helpless creepy walrus. Complete chaos, nobody knowing what to do but everybody giving suggestions. They point at the arms of the chair, suggesting that they be hacked off. The face of the warden explodes: "What! Destroy my chair!"

Others suggest that he be stripped naked, that maybe he'd be less fat in his birthday suit; others suggest he be placed in the chair sideways; and others that he sit with his feet up on the chair. Each suggestion is enacted visually by the suggestor.

The prisoner is trying to help squeeze himself in—he is embarrassed because he is giving them such a hard time. Suddenly the executioner (not one to be denied) comes up with a brainstorm: let him sit on the arms of the chair; it's not the seat that jolts them but the headpiece and the ankle straps and the arm straps, and if the ankle straps were not possible, then the headpiece and arm straps would be enough. He'd make sure they'd be enough, like he'd give the elephant the juiciest jolt ever.

And the music gets wilder and faster and louder, and now the guards and warden are real bugged, angry as all get-out: they hate the miserable bastard for screwing up the works. They roughly get him to sit on the arms.

The poor fat man begins to cry. Like wild-eyed insane ducks the guards and warden and executioner attempt to strap his feet and cap his head, but no dice: his feet can't reach the straps and his head is high over the metal cap; now the warden begins to cry too. A sad absurd mess, the whole scene, a lousy miserable mess.

The warden calls a halt to the hysteria. He picks up a phone and calls for a carpenter; obviously he gets an affirmative answer. He has the solution. He explains to the assembled onlookers how it will work. As the carpenter arrives, the warden seats himself in the "chair." "Since it is just a matter of a few inches in width in the 'chair,' this arm can be taken off and moved over six inches by attaching it to an extension." He is demonstrating to the carpenter as he talks. As further demonstration, he attaches to himself the headpiece and the wrist straps to show that there is enough slack in the wiring to allow for the extension. The carpenter is following his every move.

The carpenter, burdened with a small plank and his box of tools, bends down to measure the seat of the chair—and without looking, hands the plank and the tools to the person immediately behind him. The person happens to be the priest, who now finds himself burdened with the paraphernalia, looks for somebody to hand it to and discovers they are all on the other side of the chair supervising the reconstruction.

The priest, who has always seen himself as an assistant to the "Carpenter of Nazareth," now finds himself an assistant to the carpenter of Sing Sing. He becomes interested in the construction, particularly since the carpenter is calling for the various tools he needs. In the process of passing the tools to the carpenter, the Bible in the priest's hands becomes awkward to manipulate. To ease his burden he reaches backward and places the Bible on a small shelf that is, in actuality, the top of the electrical box that controls the juice for the "chair." Protruding from the face of the box in a perpendicular-to-the-wall position is the lever which activates the electricity. In its straight-out position it is OFF.

The carpenter continues calling for tools, and finally he asks for the plank. The priest raises the plank to hand it to the carpenter and in doing so strikes the side of the electrical box. CUT of the box as we see the Bible totter—then with a very definite movement the Bible falls forward and strikes the lever, slamming it ON. As we CUT instantly to the warden, who is strapped into the chair and is now writhing with the jolt of 200,000 volts of electricity, two guards, in panic, try to pull his arms from the wrist straps, and upon contact with him they too are electrocuted. The other two guards try to pull them from the electrical force that has welded them to the warden, and they too become part of this unbreakable electrical death chain. The chain continues, with the executioner and the carpenter making contact with the "group." The carpenter reaches out his free hand in supplicatlon to the priest—who takes his hand . . . and dies also.

In a wide-angle view of the room, as the electricity continues to crackle through the writhing bodies of the eight electrocuted men, only the condemned prisoner stands alive—and alone!

He looks at the scene for a moment, walks slowly to where the Bible is lying on the floor, picks it up, dusts it off, opens it, and, immersed in reading, walks toward and through the Little Black Door.

FADE OUT

Acknowledgments

Profound thanks are extended to the following for their generous financial support which helped to defray some of this book's production costs:

Theo Alpert, Micah Altman, Adrian Astur Álvarez, Rune Andersen, Robert W Archambault, Paul E. Bach, Jr., Thomas Young Barmore Jr, Steven Belletto, Cameron Bennett, Grant Biven, Matthew Boe, Brian R. Boisvert, Daniel Buckle, Chris Call, Tobias Carroll, Scott Chiddister, Jerry Cimino, Chelsea Clifton, C. Colla, Jonathan Collins, Jangus C. Cooper, Malcolm & Parker Curtis, Frank Derfield Jr, Brian Dupre, V.J. Eaton, Curtis B. Edmundson, Isaac Ehrlich, John Feins, Raymond Foye, Justin Gallant, GMarkC, The Godenho Whanau, Damian Gordon, Adam Greenfield, Wesley Hoffman, Kaarina Hollo, Tamsin Hollo, Neil Glenn Jacobson, Brian Jagodzinski, Erik T Johnson, Fred W Johnson, Haya .K., Gautham Kalva, Terry Kattleman, Handsome Ryan Kennedy, Jack Kerns, Paul Kuliev, Mark Lamb, Cari Liebenberg, Chris Linton, Luzius, Sheri Lynne, Brian de León Macchiarelli, Jonathan Mack, Elizabeth Maxim, Jim McElroy, Donald McGowan, Jack Mearns, Dr. Melvin "Steve" Mesophagus, Kenneth Morris, Geoffrey Moses, Gregory Moses, Séamus Murphy, Michael O'Shaughnessy, Dan Pack,

Alfie Palao, Kelly Harshfield Pavlik, Andrew Pearson, Poems-For-All, Pedro Ponce, Waylon M. Prince, Nicholas Grendel Rabinowicz, Walter Raubicheck, Patrick M Regner, Benjamin Riddle, Taren JFKDR Robinson, Jessica Rosen, Frank V. Saltarelli, Ben Schafer, Brant Shapiro, Adrianna Liberty Skillin, Sid Sondergard, Martin E Stein & Scott A Saxon, K.L. Stokes, William Stokes, S.W. Thompson, Laki Vazakas, Jack Waters, William Waters, Rachel Wells, Isaiah Whisner, Charles Wilkins, David S Wills, T.R. Wolfe, The Zemenides Family, and Anonymous

www.ingramcontent.com/pod-product-compliance
Lightning Source LLC
Chambersburg PA
CBHW011509100726
47900CB00009B/2665

* 9 7 8 0 5 7 8 7 7 7 0 1 6 *